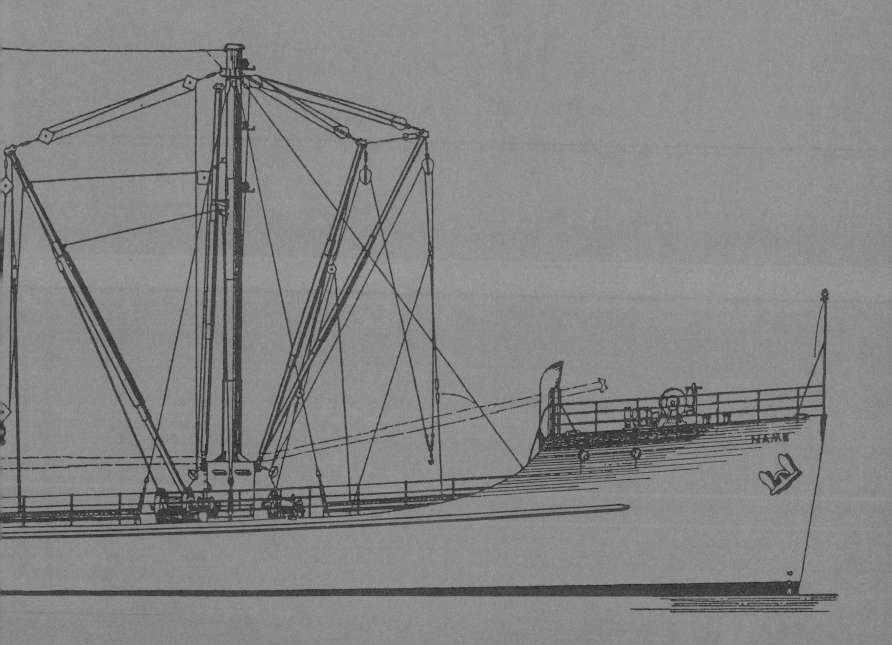

1947: *The Alaska waterborne traffic picture is unique inasmuch as it is highly seasonal in nature, a "one-way" proposition without benefit of back-haul, and has a period in the dead of winter during which the needs of the Territory can be served through use of only a minor part of the freight and passenger tonnage required to maintain service during spring, summer and fall months.*[1]

– Admiral F. A. Zeusler, U.S. Coast Guard (Ret.)

• • •

1962: *The great distances and small tonnage available present a unique problem to any carrier. Probably nowhere else in the world does a private common carrier operate in a trade that provides him with less than one ton of cargo for every mile traveled. In addition there are the inherent hazards of the operation, such as one-way haul, seasonality, and the number of small ports. This pattern of maritime carriers coming and going in the Alaska trade over the years has worked a real hardship on all concerned. Each one of them has skimmed some of the cream off the trade and many of them have assumed little or no responsibility. Meanwhile this surviving common carrier [Alaska Steamship] has been left to provide the reliable service that the Alaskan economy requires.*[2]

– D. E. Skinner, Alaska Steamship Company

• • •

1980: *Alaska's transportation needs are unique compared to those of the contiguous states. This uniqueness results from a small population being scattered across a vast, rugged area, mostly in urban coastal centers. These centers either have no highway connections to the outside or can be served by overland transportation only at considerable expense. Consequently, the dominant modes of transport in Alaska are air and marine, precisely those that play the smallest role in the domestic commerce of the contiguous states.*[3]

– John Gray, economist

ALEUTIAN FREIGHTER

A History of Shipping in the Aleutian Islands

James Mackovjak

Documentary Media

Seattle

Aleutian Freighter
A History of Shipping in the Aleutian Islands

First Edition 2012

Printed in Canada

Author: James Mackovjak
Editor: Judy Gouldthorpe
Project Manager: Capt. George Collazo, Coastal Transportation, Inc.
Designer: Marilyn Esguerra, Philips Publishing Group
Publisher: Petyr Beck
Producer: Peter Strong, owner, Coastal Transportation, Inc.

ISBN: 978-1-933245-27-0

Library of Congress Cataloging-in-Publication Data

Mackovjak, James R.
Aleutian freighter : a history of shipping in the Aleutian Islands / James Mackovjak. – 1st ed.
     p. cm.
Includes bibliographical references.
ISBN 978-1-933245-27-0 (alk. paper)
1. Shipping–Alaska–Aleutian Islands–History. I. Title.
HE752.A4M33 2012
387.5'44097984–dc23
                    2012011321

Philips Publishing Group

Book Design by: Philips Publishing Group
www.philipspublishing.com

Published by: Documentary Media LLC
3250 41st Avenue SW, Seattle, Washington 98116
(206) 935-9292 | email: books@docbooks.com
www.documentarymedia.com

Contents

Foreword

THROUGHOUT MY LIFE, I HAVE WORKED IN MANY PLACES, RANGING FROM REMOTE CONSTRUCTION SITES IN ALASKA TO CAPITOL HILL. Yet, I recall with fond memories my time as a licensed captain operating tugboats and delivering supplies to communities up and down the Yukon River. I have always had a warm spot in my heart for seafarers, especially those fishermen and traders who sail in the Aleutian Islands and surrounding areas. The menacing skies, perilous currents, and dangerous seas that they encounter would be enough to terrify anyone. They work, day and night, in weather fair and foul, in waters that are arguably among the most treacherous on the planet. These men and women deserve an enormous amount of our respect.

The importance of their effort cannot be overstated. Consider the fisheries: Over half of all the seafood caught in the United States comes from Alaska's waters, and a major portion of Alaska's production comes from the Aleutian Islands area. The catch, which includes salmon, crab, halibut, cod, and pollock, provides American families with wholesome, nutritious food and helps power our export market.

The development of commercial fisheries in the Aleutian Islands area, however, has not been easy. Ensuring that there is a sustainable supply of seafood and protecting our resources from foreign fishermen has been the result of long legislative battles. The passage in 1976 of the Magnuson-Stevens Fishery Conservation and Management Act, which was later amended by my good friend Senator Stevens, was a major step in getting Alaska's fisheries on track. With this legislation, the United States took jurisdiction of our seas out to 200 miles from our coastline, which put an end to the ravages of unregulated foreign fishing fleets and fostered the development of a domestic fleet and sustainable fisheries.

Prior to the 1970s, the Aleutian Islands lacked sufficient infrastructure to be considered economically viable. There were few docks and cold-storage facilities, but more important, there was no regional hub or center for processing the fish that were caught. The contrast with today could not be starker. When you visit Dutch Harbor, you are confronted by a bustling and thriving fishing port that is the largest, in volume terms, in the United States. In 2010, fishing vessels delivered 515 million pounds of seafood that had a dockside value of $163 million. Dutch Harbor, with the other fishing ports in the region, is a key element of Alaska's economy.

Fishermen are not the only people plying these waters. Those who live and conduct business in the Aleutian Islands, in the Pribilof Islands, and along the Alaska Peninsula's coast have long relied on ships and boats of all kinds to provide them with everyday supplies. In the early years, mailboats were the region's primary link to the rest of the world, carrying, in addition to the mail, passengers and a wide variety of cargo—even Christmas trees. As the fishing industry developed, small cargo vessels that served the industry began carrying general cargo to and from the region's widely dispersed communities.

To ensure that this vital service was maintained, I authored what is known as the Aleutian Trade Act, which was passed by Congress in 1990. The legislation formally authorizes qualified fishing-industry vessels to transport general cargo in the Aleutian Islands area, which includes as well the Pribilof Islands and ports on the Alaska Peninsula. By all measures, the Aleutian Trade Act has been a success in fostering safe and reliable cargo service throughout the region, and I am proud of it.

Knowledge of Alaska's rich history is fundamental to shaping decisions that we will make in the future. Understanding the history of the Aleutian Islands region, its people, and their industries is not only important for Alaskans, it is vital for all Americans. I want to thank Jim Mackovjak for documenting the history of maritime trade in this area, and to recognize the support for the project that was provided by Peter Strong, of Coastal Transportation. This book is an invaluable record that will be appreciated for many years to come by students of Alaska's history.

In closing, I want to wish smooth passage to the vessels and people who ply Alaska's waters. My thoughts are with them all.

Stay safe,

Rep. Don Young
Congressman for All Alaska

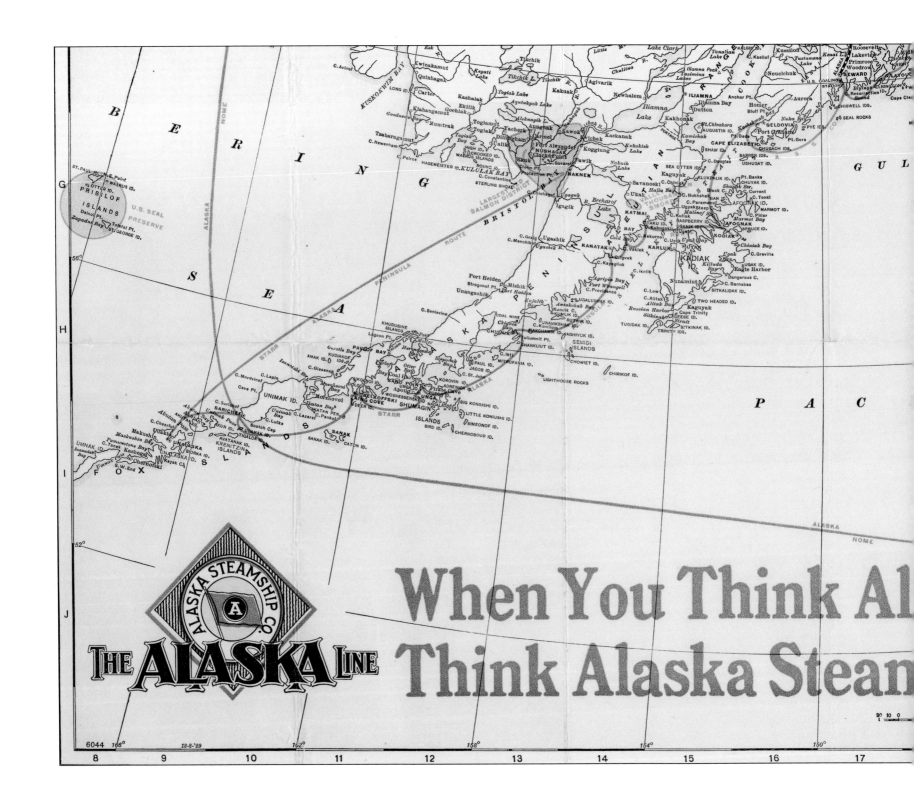

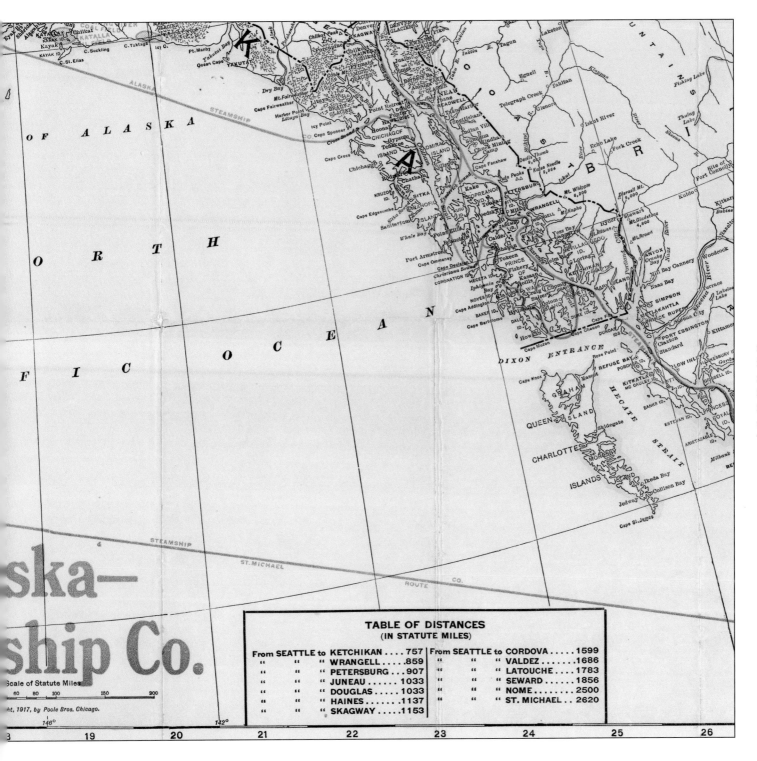

Section of Alaska Steamship Company map showing Southwest and Southeast Alaska routes, 1917.

TABLE OF DISTANCES
(IN STATUTE MILES)

From SEATTLE to			From SEATTLE to		
"	"	KETCHIKAN 757	"	"	CORDOVA 1599
"	"	WRANGELL .... .859	"	"	VALDEZ 1686
"	"	PETERSBURG ... 907	"	"	LATOUCHE 1783
"	"	JUNEAU 1033	"	"	SEWARD 1856
"	"	DOUGLAS 1033	"	"	NOME 2500
"	"	HAINES 1137	"	"	ST. MICHAEL .. 2620
"	"	SKAGWAY 1153			

Scale of Statute Miles
60 80 100   150   200

...ht, 1917, by Poole Bros. Chicago.

Coastal Nomad in ice alongside the dock at St. Paul, Pribilof Islands.

The Aleutian Islands and Lower Alaska Peninsula Area: Geography, Weather, and Resources

Left to Right:
Crew of the Western Pioneer freighter *Sculpin*, her deck covered with ice, circa 1980s.

Fishermen handle pollock aboard a Bering Sea trawler.

The *Sculpin* in pack ice.

THE TERM ALEUTIAN TRADE AS USED IN THIS WORK REFERS TO THE MARITIME TRANSPORT OF FREIGHT between Puget Sound, in Washington State, and the lower Alaska Peninsula and Aleutian Islands region of Alaska, including the Pribilof Islands.

As regards commercial transportation, the Alaska Peninsula is for all intents and purposes an island. No roads connect it to Alaska's road system; transportation is limited to air and sea. The Aleutian trade is today primarily based on supporting the vast seafood industry that has developed in the region over the last six decades. Supplies for every facet of the industry, along with general cargo to support the area's population, are transported north in vessels that return south laden with frozen seafood. An impediment to commerce in the region is its remoteness and lack of services. Such services as are available are centered in Dutch Harbor, the principal port in the Aleutian Islands. "Dutch," as it is called,

is nearly 800 air miles from Anchorage and some 1,800 sea (nautical) miles from Seattle, and offers fuel and some supply and repair services. It also has scheduled daily air service from Anchorage. The waters of the Aleutian Islands/lower Alaska Peninsula region are among the most hazardous on Earth, particularly during the winter. The waters of the Gulf of Alaska, which must be traversed as part of the trade, are likewise extremely formidable.

THE ALEUTIAN ISLANDS AND LOWER ALASKA PENINSULA

The rugged Alaska Peninsula arcs in a southwesterly direction from near the southwest corner of Alaska's mainland mass. It is some 500 miles long and 40 miles wide. The peninsula is volcanic in origin and remains volcanically active. The western shore of the Alaska Peninsula is the Bering Sea, including Bristol Bay, which hosts the largest salmon run in

Crewmember re-securing deck cargo on Western Pioneer Company vessel *Dolphin* in heavy seas.

BERING SEA

Ships that operate in the Bering Sea . . . are presumed to operate in a semi-submerged condition.
— Coastal Transportation, Inc. *Vessel Operation Manual*, 2006[4]

The Bering Sea, a northern extension of the North Pacific Ocean, is a semi-enclosed subarctic sea that encompasses some 878,000 square miles. In the north it is separated from the Chukchi Sea by the Bering Strait. It is bordered on the east by the mainland coast of the United States (Alaska), and on the west by the mainland coast of Russia. The southern boundary of the Bering Sea is an arc that runs along the Alaska Peninsula and through the Aleutian and Commander Islands to Cape Kamchatka. The sea is named for Vitus Bering, the Danish navigator who, in the employ of the Russian government, initially explored it in 1728.

Much of the eastern Bering Sea is underlain by the continental shelf, with its waters generally less than 80 fathoms deep. The waters of the western Bering Sea, on the other hand, tend to be deep, with some locations exceeding 1,900 fathoms.

The Bering Sea's weather is governed largely by the Aleutian Low, a semistationary low-pressure center that is located near the Islands.[b][5] It is most intense during the winter months. The 2007 *Coast Pilot*, the U.S. government's guide to maritime navigation, describes weather conditions in the Bering Sea as being "generally bad and very changeable." Good weather is an exception, and tends to be of short duration when it does occur. While the summer season is characterized by fog and considerable rain, winter, according to the *Coast Pilot*, is a "time of almost continuous storminess."[6] Sustained winds of 60 to 75 knots are not uncommon during storms, and winds may exceed 100 knots in severe storms. The waves generated in severe storms may be 40 to 50 feet high, although higher waves have been reported.[7] Dutch Harbor, in particular, is subject during the winter to *williwaws*—violent gusts of wind that sweep down off mountain slopes with great force.[8] During a storm

the world. There are few protected harbors on the Bering Sea side of the lower Alaska Peninsula, which has greatly limited the establishment of shore-based seafood processing plants. The Alaska Peninsula's island-studded eastern shore is bounded (north to south) by Cook Inlet, Shelikof Strait, and the Gulf of Alaska. From Chignik south there are numerous bays and sheltered locations, some of which are home to modern shore-based seafood processing plants.

The Aleutian Islands are geologically a 1,100-mile continuation of the Alaska Peninsula. The Chain, as the Aleutians are often referred to, is composed of more than 300 treeless volcanic islands that are snow-covered and windblown during the winter and often shrouded in fog during the summer. Protected harbors are few and far between. Unimak Pass, at the north end of the Aleutians, is on the Great Circle Route between the U.S. West Coast and the Far East, and is annually transited by some 4,500 cargo vessels.[a]

---

a   The Alaska Peninsula and Aleutian Islands are part of the Pacific Ring of Fire, a geologically and volcanically active band that nearly encircles the Pacific Ocean basin.

b   The community of Unalaska bills itself as the "Birthplace of the Winds."

in December 1988, a fishing vessel in Dutch Harbor clocked winds of 150 knots.[9]

Particularly when heavy seas are combined with sub-freezing air temperatures, vessels are vulnerable to superstructure icing that at a minimum hampers deck activity. In severe situations, it can result in significantly reduced freeboard and a dangerous loss of stability. Because of their lower freeboard and greater motion in the water, smaller vessels are particularly vulnerable to superstructure icing. Icing is an ever-present danger during the winter months and has claimed a number of vessels and lives.

Tidal currents in all Aleutian Islands passes are strong. In the narrow Akun Strait (between Akutan and Akun Islands), the current may reach 12 knots.[10] At the entrances to passes, waves moving in opposition to currents "stack up"— become higher and closer together—which sometimes poses a hazard to vessels. The maximum tidal range at Unalaska/Dutch Harbor is about six feet.

A major impediment to commercial fishing and other activities in the Bering Sea is the ice that forms during the winter over the sea's northern reaches. The ice endures well into spring. Rather than being a solid sheet, however, it tends to drift in detached fields, floes, and cakes. The approximate southern boundary of the ice runs from Bristol Bay to St. George Island, the southernmost of the Pribilof Islands, then west-northwest to the Siberian shore.[11]

The Bering Sea is a biological treasure-house of the first magnitude in terms of both diversity and volume. It is home to at least 450 species of fish, crustaceans, and mollusks, about 25 of which have commercial value. In addition, there are 50 species of seabirds and 25 species of marine mammals.[12] The broad continental shelf of the eastern region of the Bering Sea is particularly rich, and it contains what some estimate to be more than 20 percent of the world's fisheries resources.[13]

Harvesting and processing seafood is the core industry of this region. The industry that has developed is fairly diverse, but seasonal in nature. Like all fisheries, it is subject to a host of variables that include changes in fish stocks, market conditions, environmental considerations, and raw politics. The fisheries of the U.S. waters of the Bering Sea are administered by the National Marine Fisheries Service (NMFS), a branch of the Department of Commerce. The

U.S. Coast Guard regularly patrols the Bering Sea. It enforces vessel safety regulations, maintains aids to navigation, and assists in the enforcement of fisheries regulations.

In terms of the poundage of fish landed, Dutch Harbor has ranked first among U.S. seafood ports for two decades. In 2007, landings totaled some 777 million pounds and had an ex-vessel value of $174 million.[14] The landings included a variety of species, among them walleye pollock, Pacific cod, yellowfin sole, Atka mackerel, halibut, salmon, and king and snow crabs.

Most of the landings were walleye pollock (*Theragra chalcogramma*), a large-headed, bulbous-eyed, white-fleshed fish that averages about 14 inches long.[c] The flesh of the relatively fast-growing pollock is high in protein and low in carbohydrates and fat. It is the raw material for fast-food fish sandwiches and frozen fish sticks, as well as surimi, a fish paste made from the ground-up flesh of white-meated fish that has long been a staple of the Japanese diet.

The pollock fishery in the Bering Sea and Aleutian Islands constitutes the largest fishery in the world, and annual harvests, though currently declining, have been in the 1.1 million metric ton range. By weight, approximately 30 percent of all fish landed in the United States are pollock from the Bering Sea/Aleutian Islands fishery.[15] The annual value of the Alaska pollock catch, after processing, is some $1 billion.[16]

GULF OF ALASKA'S SOUTHWESTERN WATERS

Like the Bering Sea, the Gulf of Alaska is an extremely formidable body of water in which severe subarctic storms can persist for days, particularly during the winter. Some of the huge waves generated in these storms are more than 30 feet high, and much to the delight of surfers, these are the same waves that strike the north shore of Oahu several times each winter. Each voyage between Puget Sound and the Alaska Peninsula/Aleutian Islands area requires a crossing of the Gulf during which a vessel may be days away from a safe harbor and completely on its own. The Gulf of Alaska proper does not freeze over, but superstructure icing is often encountered.

---

c The pollock caught in the Bering Sea are not true pollock (genus *Pollachius*).

Dockworkers load wooden cases of canned salmon onto a sailing ship at Chignik. Cardboard boxes replaced wooden cases in the early 1930s.

CHAPTER 1

Early Fishing and Fur-Harvesting Efforts

ALASKA BECAME A RUSSIAN POSSESSION by right of Vitus Bering's "discovery" of the territory in 1741. In 1799, the Russian-American Company was chartered to administer and commercially exploit what was then known as "Russian America." The firm's core business revolved around obtaining pelts, particularly those of sea otters, thousands of which were harvested in the Aleutian Islands.

Alaska under the colonial management of the Russians gradually evolved into an economic liability. The population of sea otters was drastically diminished by hunting, and there was nothing on the horizon that seemed likely to replace the lost revenue.[1] Meanwhile, the costs of subsidizing—and potentially defending—the vast and remote colony continued unabated. The country's rulers therefore decided to sell the territory, but there were geopolitical considerations regarding to whom it might be offered. Unlike Great Britain, which owned the colony of British Columbia and had helped defeat Russia in the Crimean War, the United States was on good terms with Russia and posed no threat to it. As a result of these factors, the United States was the preferred customer, and the selling price was accordingly set low.

The primary motive of U.S. Secretary of State William Seward in purchasing Alaska was not to gain access to the territory's resources, but to commence the country's effort to establish a Pacific Coast empire. An ardent expansionist, Seward believed that if the United States gained control of Alaska, then British Columbia, sandwiched between Alaska and Washington Territory, might eventually be acquired by the United States as part of a natural political progression.

For its part, Congress appropriated the $7.2 million purchase price for Alaska out of economic considerations: at a bargain price that amounted to 1.9 cents per acre, the representatives of the American people—despite derogatory editorial characterizations of Alaska (e.g., "Seward's Icebox" and "Walrussia")—in large part believed that Alaska was a worthwhile investment.[2]

Nevertheless, $7.2 million was a considerable sum for a country that had only recently emerged from the long and bitter Civil War and was preoccupied with Reconstruction. How would the investment in, and cost of administering, this remote and often forbidding territory be recovered? Some were confident that the development of Alaska's resources would enable the new possession to quickly pay its own way. However, despite speculation about vast mineral wealth, there were few (and modest) proven ore deposits. And Alaska's timber, though considerable, could not compete with the vast, barely tapped stands in Washington and Oregon. The salmon that ascended Alaska's rivers in almost countless numbers also had little commercial value: Pacific Coast rivers from Puget Sound to San Francisco Bay, particularly the Columbia, provided more than could be utilized on the sparsely populated coast. Petroleum, of course, was not even a consideration in that time of coal and cordwood.

The greatest potential for promptly generating economic returns from Alaska—a potential that was soon to be realized—was not to be found in the territory's relatively hospitable regions. It was in the Bering Sea, where one resource in particular—fur seals (*Callorhinus ursinus*)—had proven value. Ironically, when the acquisition of Alaska was advocated before Congress, there was apparently no mention made of a potential trade in fur seal skins.[3]

The skins of fur seals, though not nearly as valuable as those of sea otters, had been harvested by the Russians mostly on the cold, isolated, treeless, and windblown Pribilof Islands, which were uninhabited when Vitus Bering first visited Alaska. To conduct the industry, the Russians forced Aleuts into what were essentially slave colonies on the Pribilofs. Obtaining fur seal skins was a fairly simple, though labor-

Aleut sea otter hunter and fur seals, circa 1870s.

intensive, process. Fur seals that gathered on the beaches during the mating season were driven inland toward salting stations. There they were clubbed to death, bled, and quickly skinned. The skins were then salted and held in storage until a transport vessel arrived. After some spectacularly wasteful episodes (in 1803, some 70,000 fur seal skins spoiled and were dumped into the sea), the Russians began a successful program to manage the fur seal population in a manner that approximated sustainability.[4] Approximately 42,000 fur seals were harvested annually between the years 1820 and 1867. Ivan Petroff, who reported on Alaska for the U.S. government in 1880, wrote that Russian managers had looked upon the fur seal resource as "an unfailing treasury from which to draw in times of need."[5] Such was the situation at the time when Alaska was transferred to the United States.

A second resource of proven value was also found in the Bering Sea. The humble codfish, which had for centuries been a staple food in Europe as well as North America, was found in great abundance in the waters of the eastern Bering Sea. Pioneer scientist and surveyor George Davidson, who in 1867 was part of a U.S. government geographical reconnaissance of coastal Alaska to ascertain the "most available channels of commerce," considered the Pacific cod (*Gadus macrocephalus*) "the most valuable fish on [Alaska's] coast."[6] American fishermen from San Francisco had been catching and salting Pacific cod in the Bering Sea even before Alaska became a U.S. possession. The codfish industry that developed after the United States acquired Alaska was hardly a boom, but it was the nation's first successful endeavor at commercially exploiting the territory's fisheries.

The United States formally took possession of Alaska in October 1867. The U.S. Army was given jurisdiction over the unorganized territory, but its presence was limited to a contingent of soldiers deployed at posts scattered along the coast from Dixon Entrance to Kodiak. Then, in July of 1868, Congress passed legislation that declared the entirety of Alaska to be a "customs collection district" under the jurisdiction of the Treasury Department. The legislation also authorized the Secretary of the Treasury to establish regulations by which all vessels owned by residents of Alaska could be registered as U.S. vessels ("naturalized"), and declared that the "coasting trade" (coastwise trade) between Alaska and

Drawing by H. W. Elliott.

any other portion of the United States would be regulated "in accordance with the provisions of law applicable to such trade between any two great [customs collection] districts."[7] By 1868, a customs house was established at Unalaska, in the Aleutian Islands, a location touted as the "true commercial centre of the Territory" in an 1869 government report.[8] Customs officers were authorized to enter and clear vessels and to receive duties and fees.

The Army was withdrawn from Alaska in 1877, and the Collector of Customs was put in charge by default. Two years later, jurisdiction over Alaska was transferred to the U.S. Navy. In 1884, Congress passed the Alaska Organic Act, which created the District of Alaska and provided for civil government under a governor appointed by the U.S. president.

During the administration of Theodore Roosevelt (1901-1909), the federal government sought to obtain a reliable measurement of the flow of commerce between the United States and its territories, some of which had only recently been acquired. To do so, Congress passed legislation in 1902 that became known as the Cargo Manifest Law. The legislation extended export laws to require that each vessel

Aleuts in kayaks near St. Paul, Pribilof Islands.

departing a port in the contiguous states and destined for a noncontiguous U.S. territory—including Alaska, Hawaii, Guam, and the Philippines—file a statement showing the quantity and value of all goods carried.[9] No item, no matter how insignificant, was exempted.[a] The law was unpopular among transporters, who considered the preparation of the statements to be "tedious, difficult and costly."[10] Nevertheless, the requirement remained in effect for almost a half century, until the late 1940s.

Alaska gained limited self-government when it became an official territory in 1912. Despite the passage of this law, the federal government continued its jurisdiction over commerce between the territory and the lower 48 states. To this day, maritime commerce to and from Alaska is principally regulated by federal agencies, particularly the Federal Maritime Commission and the Surface Transportation Board (successor to the Interstate Commerce Commission).

Primary Industries in the Bering Sea

FUR SEALS

In the period immediately following the transfer of Alaska to the United States, the territory's resources were basically there for the taking. In the Pribilof Islands, a free-for-all slaughter of fur seals ensued. "Marauders," mostly Russian, killed an estimated 100,000 within a year of the transfer, and additional sealing expeditions were organized.[11] The skins were purchased by Hutchinson, Kohl & Co. of San Francisco and shipped to Messrs. Lampson & Co. in London, England, to be fashioned into very expensive coats.[b][12] At that time, a raw skin delivered to London fetched about seven dollars in gold.[13] The U.S. government received no benefit from the

sealing. During the summer of 1868, Congress reacted to the slaughter by passing legislation that outlawed the killing of any fur seal.[14] Word of the ban was slow to spread, and the killing continued unabated until late fall.[15] Among the businesses involved in killing seals on St. Paul Island that summer was Hutchinson, Kohl & Co. At Northeast Point alone, Hutchinson, Kohl and the Connecticut firm Williams & Haven reportedly killed some 75,000 young male fur seals. The killing ceased only because the work crews were completely exhausted and had run out of salt, which was used to preserve the skins.[16]

The following year, Congress declared the Pribilof Islands to be a "special reservation for government purposes" and stipulated that, until otherwise provided by law, no person was permitted to land or remain on the islands without permission of the Secretary of the Treasury.[17] Customs Inspector Joseph Wilson traveled from San Francisco to the Pribilof Islands aboard the steamer *Alexander* and took possession of the islands for the federal government. Not long after Wilson's arrival, the bark *Monticello*, laden with trading goods from Honolulu, arrived at St. Paul. The vessel departed after government agents informed its master that he lacked permission to land his cargo.[18]

Despite the previous year's ban on killing fur seals, Secretary of the Treasury George Boutwell authorized the harvesting of some 42,000 fur seals to provide "sustenance and clothing" to the Aleuts who inhabited the islands. Hutchinson, Kohl & Co. purchased the skins.[19] Customs Inspector Wilson valued that year's fur seal skin harvest at over a half million dollars, and suggested that the revenue accruing from them, if garnered by the U.S. government, would itself in 12 or 13 years refund the entire amount paid for Alaska. He believed that the fur seal resource, properly conserved, would be a "source of endless revenue" for the U.S. Treasury.[20] His estimation was optimistic, but not overly so. By 1897, 30 years after Alaska was purchased, total income from fur seals had exceeded the $7.2 million purchase price.[21]

In purchasing Alaska, the United States explicitly accepted responsibility for the region's Native people. Of the Aleuts residing on the Pribilof Islands, Secretary Boutwell acknowledged that the government "is bound to protect the people in the enjoyment of their only means of subsistence"—

---

a   The Cargo Manifest Law required each bill of lading to be accompanied by a notarized export declaration showing the amount, description, and value of every article shipped. As well, each article had to be classified according to a code that delineated 1,776 item types. The September 1939 sailing of the Alaska Steamship Co's *Aleutian* required 3,120 individual export declarations. One firm in the Alaska trade reported that it had filed more than 400,000 declarations in 1940. The direct economic burden of this requirement borne by those in the Alaska trade at that time was estimated to be about $75,000 annually.

b   Other garments manufactured from fur seal skins were hats, jackets, carriage robes, and muffs.

Sea otter hunters and kayaks. Note waterproof garments and the kayaks' waterproof "skirts," which are drawn snug around seated kayakers to prevent rain and seawater from entering the vessel.

fur seals. Boutwell suggested that government should "manage the business" of obtaining fur seal skins. If this failed, the "fishery" could be leased to a private concern.[22] The Alaska Commercial Co. (informally known as "Alaska Commercial") was organized specifically to obtain such a lease. Alaska Commercial had its roots in the Russian-American Co. In the months following the transfer of Alaska to the United States, Hayward M. Hutchinson of Hutchinson, Kohl & Co. in San Francisco purchased the Russian-American Co.'s remaining assets in the territory, including its buildings, ships, and equipment. Hutchinson, Kohl & Co. was in turn purchased in 1868 by San Francisco merchants Lewis Gerstle and Louis Sloss, who formed the Alaska Commercial Company, which remains in business in Alaska to this day.[23]

Congress, reportedly as a result of some untoward lobbying by individuals representing the Alaska Commercial Co., decided that the best course of action was to lease the Pribilof Islands. On July 1, 1870, Congress passed the Act to Prevent the Extermination of Fur-bearing Animals in Alaska. The legislation stipulated that for the next 20 years, the annual harvest of fur seals on the Pribilof Islands would be limited to 75,000 on St. Paul Island and 25,000 on St. George Island.

In addition, Congress directed the Secretary of the Treasury to lease the Pribilofs "to proper and responsible parties, to the best advantage of the United States." Congress stipulated that the minimum lease price be $50,000 per year and that a "revenue tax or duty" of two dollars be collected on each skin shipped from the islands.[24] The U.S. government awarded the Alaska Commercial Co. the exclusive 20-year right to harvest fur seals in Alaska. The cost was $50,000, plus $2.625 for each skin taken or shipped from the Pribilof Islands. As part of the contract, the Alaska Commercial Co. was required to secure permission from the federal government each time it intended to send a vessel to the Pribilofs.[25]

Two vessels, each with similar capacity, were initially employed by the Alaska Commercial Co. in its Pribilof operations. One was the steamer *Alexander*, and the other was the *Cyane*, a sailing vessel. Goods were generally transported aboard the *Cyane* from San Francisco to Unalaska, where the company maintained storage facilities. The *Alexander* plied the waters of the Bering Sea, transporting supplies from Unalaska to the Pribilofs and returning with fur seal skins. At the end of the season, both the *Alexander* and the *Cyane* transported seal skins to San Francisco.[26] These vessels were soon augmented by the steamer *Constantine* and the schooner *H. M. Hutchinson*, both owned by the Alaska Commercial Co.[27] The steamships *St. Paul* and *Dora*, also company-owned, were later utilized in the Alaska Commercial Co.'s operation in the Pribilofs, as were the schooners *St. George* and *Matthew Turner*.[28]

Neither St. Paul nor St. George had harbors. Cargo, therefore, was laboriously lightered between the shore and vessels anchored at some distance (often a mile or more) in oar-powered skin boats called *baidars*. These open vessels were constructed of a wood frame covered with sea lion skins.

They were approximately 30 feet long, had a beam of about eight feet, weighed around 900 pounds, and could normally carry about two tons of cargo. The unloading/loading process, particularly when the sea was rough, could take a considerable number of days. There were also labor issues. Aleut sealers on the Pribilofs were described by government agent Ivan Petroff in 1884 as "proud of their accomplishments as sealers, and too proud to demean themselves in doing any other kind of work." This included unloading and loading cargo vessels. For this job, the Alaska Commercial Co. found it necessary to bring in men from the Aleutian Islands, who were generally paid at the rate of a dollar a day. Sealers, on the other hand, were paid $0.40 cash for each seal killed, skinned, and salted.[29] A sealer earned an average of about $500 annually.[30]

Upon the expiration of the Alaska Commercial Co.'s 20-year lease on the Pribilof Islands in the spring of 1890, a new 20-year lease was awarded to the North American Commercial Co. The annual fee was $60,000 plus $2.625 for each skin taken or shipped from the islands. Unfortunately, the seal population on the Pribilofs had declined precipitously, and the total annual harvest was reduced to less than 10,000. The decline was blamed on "pelagic" hunters who indiscriminately shot seals in the open water and saved only those with marketable skins. At one point in 1891, there were between 20,000 and 30,000 dead seal pups on St. Paul Island. They were believed to have died of starvation after their mothers were killed while feeding at sea.[31] It was estimated that a total of four seals died for each marketable skin obtained as a result of losses from shot seals sinking before they could be retrieved, the discarding of shot seals with nonmarketable skins, and the starvation of pups.[32] Pelagic sealing peaked in 1894, the same year that a treaty between the United States and Great Britain prohibited the killing of fur seals within a zone 60 miles around the Pribilof Islands.[33] In 1897, Congress passed legislation that made it illegal for American persons and American vessels to engage in pelagic sealing in the Pacific Ocean north of 35 degrees north latitude (the approximate latitude of Los Angeles, California).[34]

Between 1890 and 1910, the North American Commercial Co. used its steamships *Arago*, *Farallon*, *Bertha*, and *Lakme* to transport supplies and the meager harvest of seal skins between the Pribilofs and San Francisco. Additionally, several hundred seal skins were transported from the Pribilofs in 1890 by the U.S. Revenue Cutter *Rush*.[35]

The North American Commercial Co.'s lease on the Pribilof Islands expired in 1910. It was not renewed. Instead, Congress passed what became commonly known as the Alaska Fur Seal Act, which declared the Pribilofs to be a "special reservation for government purposes." The government took charge of all matters pertaining to the Pribilofs such that, short of an emergency, it was unlawful for any person to land or remain on the islands without the permission of the secretary of commerce and labor. The legislation stipulated that only Natives would be allowed to kill and cure fur seals, and it gave the secretary of commerce and labor the "authority to furnish food, shelter, fuel, clothing, and other necessaries

Copyright, 1911, By Thwaites, J.E. 590 — Revenue Cutter, Rush, In Bering Sea, Photo. From Deck of Mail Steamer, Dora.

The Revenue Cutter *Rush* was originally constructed in 1874 and was refitted and lengthened in 1885 for service in Alaska, where one of her primary duties was to protect U.S. sealing interests. The Revenue Cutter Service was the predecessor of the U.S. Coast Guard.

of life to the native inhabitants of the Pribilof Islands and to provide for their comfort, maintenance, education and protection." The secretary was also given the authority to establish supply depots on the islands, and to transport supplies on government or privately chartered vessels.[36] The following year the U.S. government became party to the North Pacific Sealing Convention, an agreement between the United States, Japan, Russia, and Great Britain (Canada) that significantly reformed sealing. Pelagic sealing was outlawed and, in exchange, provision was made to share the seal furs produced on the Pribilofs with Japan and Great Britain.[c] The United States managed the Pribilof fur seal population and its harvest, and it kept 70 percent of the skins. The Japanese and British divided the remainder equally.[37]

Over the years 1911 through 1918, the U.S. government utilized a combination of privately chartered and military vessels to transport supplies and fur seal skins. Among the vessels chartered were the *Homer* (charter cost was $150

per day), *Melville Dollar*, *Nero*, *Elihu Thomson*, *Roosevelt*, and *Belvedere*. The government vessels utilized included the revenue cutters *Bear* and *Manning*, the Bureau of Fisheries steamer *Roosevelt*, and the U.S. Navy collier *Saturn*.[38]

The Bureau of Fisheries vessel *Eider* was brought into service in 1919 specifically to facilitate transportation to the Pribilofs. It was the former *Idaho*, a schooner constructed in 1913 to work the offshore halibut fishery. The *Eider*, powered by a 3-cylinder, 110-horsepower Frisco Standard engine that burned distillate (similar to gasoline, but less refined), was 88 feet long, with a beam of 19 feet and a draft (fully loaded) of 9 feet.[39] While the vessel occasionally transported goods to and from Seattle, mostly it shuttled between Unalaska and the Pribilofs. In 1920 the *Eider* was the first vessel ever to make a dead-of-winter voyage to the Pribilof Islands.[40] In 1923 the vessel's Frisco Standard was replaced by a 140-horsepower Atlas diesel engine.[41]

Baidars continued to be the vessel-of-choice to lighter cargo between shore and vessels that anchored offshore. Because of rough sea conditions in 1914, it took fully 23 days

c   This was the first international treaty for the protection of a marine resource.

to unload the steamer *Melville Dollar*.[42] Under especially calm conditions in 1917, however, several loads of eight and a half tons were transported. Ward Bower and Henry Aller, agents for the Bureau of Fisheries, had great respect for the baidar. They thought it somewhat surprising that for lightering supplies ashore at the Pribilofs, no modern contrivance could match this "primitive native boat."[43] Nevertheless, there were calls for a modern solution to the problem, including the installation at St. Paul and St. George Islands of aerial cable systems running from shore to a large buoy moored about 1,500 feet offshore.[44]

In 1928, Congress appropriated $125,000 to replace the *Eider*, which "on account of its age and the severe service in which it has been used," was to be assigned to do patrol work in less-exposed waters.[45]

The *Eider*'s replacement, the *Penguin*, was constructed at Ballard Marine Railway (Seattle) and launched on January 8, 1930. With a length of 130 feet and a beam of 27 feet, she was the largest of the Bureau of Fisheries Alaska vessels.

The vessel was stoutly constructed largely of Alaska cedar (yellow cedar) and sheathed for protection against ice. A 400-horsepower Union Diesel main engine provided a cruising speed of 10 knots. The *Penguin* had sleeping accommodations for 18 passengers, could carry 160 tons of cargo, and had a range of 4,000 miles. *Marine Digest*, the Seattle-based weekly journal of Pacific Northwest maritime activity, praised the *Penguin* as "one of the finest wooden vessels built in the Pacific Northwest." In the years prior to World War II and for several years after the war, the *Penguin* annually made four to six round trips between Seattle and the Pribilof Islands, logging about 29,000 miles each year in doing so.[46]

CODFISH

Salted codfish has been a staple food in Europe and North America since medieval times. It is said that tight-lipped Basque fishermen were regularly fishing the rich cod banks off the northeast coast of North America even before Christopher Columbus's time.[47] The U.S. commercial fishing industry began in colonial New England some four centuries ago and soon became a mainstay of the regional economy. Cape Cod, on the Massachusetts coast, was named in honor of the cod in 1602. Gloucester, Massachusetts, became, and for many years remained, the nation's leading seaport, due mostly to landings of Atlantic cod (*Gadus morhua*).

Shortly after gold was discovered in California, East Coast merchants began shipping even the most basic of commodities (ice was one) around Cape Horn to San Francisco. Delivered to San Francisco, salted Atlantic cod were worth, in the words of Massachusetts Senator Charles Sumner, "not less than 12 cents a pound."[48] The fishery that developed in Alaska was an effort to tap into the growing California market.

There were two components to the early Pacific cod fishery in the Aleutian Islands area. The first was the high-seas fishery. In it, a fleet of mostly San Francisco-based sailing vessels—each with a crew of 10 to 18 men, 3 to 6 dories, and a supply of salt—journeyed to the Bering Sea.[49] Cod were caught from the dories on handlines and then transferred to the sailing vessels to be butchered, salted, and stored. Transit and fishing combined, each trip lasted nearly three months.[50] These operations were precursors to those of modern-day floating processors and catcher/processors.

The amount of salted cod the fleet delivered to the San Francisco market in 1866 was estimated to be from 800 to 1,000 tons, which had a value of 7.5 to 13 cents (gold) per pound.[51] This seemed to be more than enough to end the importation of cod from the Atlantic, and in what was likely the first exportation of seafood from Alaska, one vessel delivered its entire cargo to Australia.[52]

The second component of the fishery was shore-based. Salting stations were located in protected bays near the fishing grounds. Fish were caught by dorymen and processed ashore. Other than Unalaska, there were few protected bays in close proximity to cod banks in the Bering Sea. The shore-based fishery, therefore, was centered around the Shumagin Islands, on the southeast coast of the Alaska Peninsula. Transporter vessels dispatched from San Francisco periodically brought supplies and took the salted fish to market. Transporters were all sail-powered until 1914, when the 145-foot power schooner *Golden State*—built specifically for the trade—was brought into service by the Union Fish Co. With her 150-horsepower distillate engine and a capacity of 500 tons of salted cod, the *Golden State* was at the time the largest motor-propelled vessel in the Pacific Coast fishing industry.

In addition to her engine, she was fully rigged as a three-masted schooner.[53]

The Alaska salt cod business in 1916 was characterized by a federal fisheries official as "very prosperous," due largely to a strong export demand. The chief export markets were the West Indies, South America, the Hawaiian Islands, and Australia.[54] The industry gradually faded, however. At the outbreak of World War II, its shore-based component was producing less than 200,000 pounds of dry salted cod annually. Though the high-seas fleet at that time was producing more than 3 million pounds annually, it managed to persist only until the middle of the 20th century.[55] The *C. A. Thayer*, the last commercial sailing ship to operate on the U.S. West Coast, made its final salt-cod trip to the Bering Sea in 1950.[56]

THE WHALING STATION AT AKUTAN

In 1911, the Alaska Whaling Co. established a whaling station at Akutan to process the blue whales that frequented the area from May to September or October. The operation was largely self-contained, with supplies and production transported on vessels operated or chartered by the company. In 1914, the station was purchased by North Pacific Sea Products, which operated it until 1917, when it was sold to the American Pacific Whaling Company. The station was closed in 1921, reopened the following year, and operated each season until being closed again in 1931. It was reopened in 1934, and operated each season until it was permanently shuttered in 1939. During World War II, the station was used by the U.S. Navy as a fueling site.[57]

Akutan whaling station, circa 1920s.

Alaska Traders' *Fern*, navigating the Lake Washington Ship Canal, circa 1940. Fifty years later, just a few yards south of where this photo was taken, Peter Strong established Salmon Bay Terminal, home to his Coastal Transportation, Inc., fleet.

CHAPTER 2

Essential Service:
Mailboats on the Seward-Nikolski Route

WHILE SUFFICIENT FOR THEIR OWN NEEDS, the transport vessels used in the fur seal, salt cod, and whaling industries did not serve the broader public need for passenger and merchandise transportation either to and from the region or within it. This need was met through the U.S. Post Office Department, which had established an Unalaska post office in 1888. During the first several years following the establishment of the post office, the mail was carried on an irregular schedule aboard vessels that happened to be traveling to the region. This arrangement was unsatisfactory, and in 1891 the department solicited bids for contracts to carry the mail on a scheduled basis (weather permitting) from Sitka to Unalaska. The route was dubbed the "fur seal route" because it was the same as that taken by the seals on the way to their breeding grounds on the Pribilof Islands. The contract was awarded to North American Commercial Co., which employed its vessels *Elsie* and *Crescent City* on the route.

In 1894, North American Commercial lost the contract to its rival, Alaska Commercial Co., which put the 112-foot wood-hulled vessel *Dora* on the route.[1] The *Dora*, which had been constructed in San Francisco in 1880, was rigged with sails that were complemented by a small steam engine.[2] The staunch little craft became one of the best-known vessels on the coast, nicknamed the Bulldog of the North because of her ability to consistently withstand often brutal conditions.[a][3] On one particularly trying voyage, the vessel's master, Patsy Anderson, snapped and returned to port in irons, with a mate at the helm. On a voyage during the winter of 1905-1906, heavy icing conditions, a shortage of coal, and rudder

and boiler problems largely disabled the *Dora*. Over a period of nearly two months, she essentially drifted from Chignik to Vancouver Island.[4] The *Dora*'s last run along the Sitka-Unalaska route was in 1898. In later years, she carried the mail between Valdez and Unalaska. The *Dora* retired from the mail service in 1918, and sank near Alert Bay, British Columbia, in 1920. She was not raised.[5]

S.S. *Starr*

Condemned yearly but still carrying on, the unsinkable Starr—plates groaning and creaking, her hold and decks overloaded and her Plimsoll marks underwater—kept right on plying her way over the longest and stormiest shipping route of any regularly commissioned line on the earth's surface.

— Jay Ellis Ransom, 1944[6]

The *Dora* was replaced by a series of small gasoline-powered vessels. The service they provided proved unsatisfactory, and in 1921 the small steamship *Starr* was awarded a four-year contract to operate a monthly mail route that originated at Seward and served about two dozen outports along the way to Unalaska.[7] Seward, at the time, was the southern terminus of the Alaska Engineering Commission railroad (later Alaska Railroad) and received scheduled Alaska Steamship Co. service from Seattle. Save several mishaps that temporarily put it out of service, the *Starr* provided what Anthony Dimond, Alaska's delegate to Congress, characterized as "reasonably adequate" passenger and freight service for 17 years.[8]

---

a   The *Dora* and the North American Commercial Co. steamer *Bertha* were known together as the "old sisters."

The steamer *Dora* was known as the "Bulldog of the North," and carried passengers, mail, and freight to outports along a route from Sitka to Unalaska. Image circa 1905-1909.

Thwaites. 1159.   The Cruiser Dora.

The 525-gross-ton steel-hulled *Starr* was constructed in Seattle in 1912 as a deepwater halibut boat for the San Juan Fishing & Packing Co., which operated a cannery at Seward from 1917 until 1930. The vessel was 131 feet long and had a beam of 26 feet. She was powered by a 3-cylinder, 650-horsepower steam engine that provided for a cruising speed of 8.5 knots. The vessel was also fitted with a mizzen sail that was hoisted when conditions permitted. The sail added a little speed and a measure of stability. All told, the *Starr* carried a crew of 21 men, all of whom had signed up for at least 10 months' service. A mail clerk traveled aboard the vessel and worked out of a specially designed mail room. The cost of operating the *Starr* was about $1,000 per day.[9]

The contracting of the *Starr* to carry the mail was heralded enthusiastically as a new age of transportation service to western Alaska. In Seattle, a reception was held aboard the vessel on the December evening before she departed for her duties in Alaska. When the *Starr* passed through Juneau, she was greeted by, among many others, Territorial Governor Scott Bone. A reporter for Juneau's *Alaska Daily Empire* wrote that all who viewed the *Starr* were "loud in their praise of her, her equipment and crew," and that "there has perhaps never been a boat come North that was better equipped with every device for safety than the *Starr*, as she has staunch lifeboats and all kinds of stormy weather equipment."[10]

As well as the mail and a large quantity of freight, the *Starr* could initially accommodate 25 steerage and 30 first-class passengers. By 1936, the steerage compartment was fitted with 10 bunk beds on each side of a long table, and often accommodated 80 men who were going to or returning from the fisheries in western Alaska. Two men would share a bunk, one using it during the day and the other during the night. Those not sleeping passed the time playing endless games of poker and sipping liquor. As befitted this Spartan accommodation, cold salt water ran from the taps.[11]

Local knowledge was of paramount importance in navigating the treacherous waters of western Alaska in those days, when charts were incomplete, aids to navigation were few, and the mariner's tools were basically limited to compass, sounding line, sextant, and chronometer. It was no surprise that the first master of the *Starr* was Captain O. A. Johansen, who had previously traveled the waters of western Alaska as master of the *Dora* and the *Bertha*.[12]

The *Starr*'s departures from Seward were scheduled to coincide with the arrival of Alaska Steamship vessels from Seattle. This provided for the prompt transfer to the *Starr* of westbound mail, passengers, and freight.[13]

Most ports served by the *Starr* were visited on both the outbound and inbound legs of the trip. The *Starr* usually left Seward crammed with freight. Cargo carried on deck included drums of oil, cased gasoline, machinery, sacked coal, and livestock such as chickens, pigs, and cows. Dynamite—packed neatly into a lifeboat—was also carried, though it was apparently illegal to transport the explosive on a ship carrying passengers. A greatly appreciated cargo on a late 1934 voyage was Christmas trees for residents of conspicuously treeless Unalaska.[14]

With luck, the round trip could be completed in 20 days, but it regularly took longer during the winter.[15] Because there were few good harbors and docks along the route, almost all mail, passengers, and freight were lightered to shore, usually in a ship's boat powered by four men with oars. By the mid 1930s, the *Starr* began carrying a small launch powered by an inboard engine.[16]

The *Starr* also functioned as a floating store, but its inventory was limited to fresh meat, eggs, and boxed chocolates. Though crewmen were forbidden to possess liquor, at least in 1936 the vessel's captain allowed one enterprising second mate to bring along a supply of cheap liquor, which was sold along the route at several times its Seward price.[17]

In 1917, a new industry was introduced to the Aleutian Islands: sheep ranching. Flocks of sheep were brought to Unalaska Island (Western Pacific Livestock Co.) and Umnak Island (Aleutian Livestock Co.). Unforeseen problems arose,

S.S. *Starr*

and despite government assistance, both endeavors went into receivership. Carlyle Eubanks, an insurance agent from Utah, purchased the Aleutian Livestock Co. at a receiver's sale in 1929. Western Pacific Livestock went bust in 1932 and was purchased several years later by Roy Bishop, of Portland, Oregon.[18] Shortly thereafter, the operation seems to have been absorbed into that of Aleutian Livestock. In 1936, some 50,000 sheep were ranging on Eubanks's ranches on Umnak and Unimak Islands, tended by half a dozen Basque shepherds.[b] The sheep were of the hardy merino breed, and lived on the range year-round. Because of what one writer described as the "eternal chill" of the Aleutian Islands, these sheep developed wool of such length and thickness that it always commanded a premium price—enough to offset the high cost of transporting it to market in Portland, Oregon.[c][19]

Eubanks relied on the *Starr* to bring supplies to Umnak and to send his product to market. John Corson recalled that the *Starr* anchored off Chernofski in 1936, and men with an oar-powered dory spent an entire night transporting tons of baled hay and cubed sheep food to the shore.[20] Regarding southbound cargo, Eubanks in 1939 stated that

b In 1939, Eubanks reported that his total flock of sheep numbered about 13,000.

c The average Aleutian Islands fleece was said to weigh some 12 pounds, about 5 pounds more than the U.S. average.

S.S. *Starr*'s appearance changed over the years. Here her stern was raised, along with other modifications.

he had shipped 225,000 pounds of wool over the previous two years.[21] The wool was packed in burlap bales that were eight feet long and four feet in diameter. Sixty such bales were transported from Umnak on one trip in 1936.[22]

Cases of canned salmon were also a seasonal staple cargo for the *Starr*. Corson wrote that the vessel's only cargo hold was near the bow, and that at Chignik it was once filled to the deck beams with canned salmon. When the *Starr* departed Chignik, her stern was high in the air, the highest draft mark on her bow—21 feet—was underwater, and her anchor flukes were scooping up water.[23] The *Starr* also transported salted cod on occasion.[24]

As noted previously, marine charts of Alaska's coastal waters were sketchy. Around 1914, William Redfield, President Woodrow Wilson's secretary of commerce, archly noted the "peculiar habits of surveying up there . . . [whereby] we have found many rocks by running merchant ships upon them."[25] The *Starr* seems to have been one of those ships. John Corson wrote that half the rocks along the vessel's route were located and named after the *Starr* struck them.[26] One chilling wireless message from the *Starr* from December 1928: "Hit rocks, bent propeller and shaft, heavily iced, mast carried away during gale of yesterday and today."[d 27]

There were also some lighter times. Sometime in the 1930s, four young Aleut men in two-hatch kayaks were said to have challenged the captain of the *Starr* to a race from Sanak to Unga, a distance of about 75 miles.[e] To the captain, it seemed an opportunity for some easy money, and he wagered $100. Others on the *Starr* joined in to wager various sums. It turned out to be a poor bet. The kayaks were sleek, light, and nimble, and in the hands of experienced paddlers, it did not take long or even much effort for them to take the lead. By the time half the distance was covered, they were so far ahead that they could not be seen from the bridge of the *Starr*. When the *Starr* arrived at Unga, the kayakers were standing on the dock. The men collected their winnings, were individually congratulated

by the captain, and then paddled back to Sanak.[28]

In the spring of 1935, the San Juan Fishing & Packing Co. sold the *Starr* to the Alaska Steamship Co., which also leased the mail contract.[29] In a report on the vessel's sale, the *Seward Gateway* took the opportunity to praise the "grand old historic mail ship" that had become an "institution" from Seward to the Aleutian Islands. The *Starr*, it said, was "destined to write new sagas of the seas and attain new heights in public service." The vessel's master, Captain Arthur Ryning, was soon replaced by his former first mate, Roy Wheeler. Wheeler was scheduled to be promptly replaced by Chris Tronsen, Ryning's first mate at the time.[30] Among Ryning's accomplishments while master of the *Starr* was twice delivering babies. On one January voyage, twins were born en route from Akutan to Unalaska.[31]

Under Alaska Steamship (and perhaps before), the *Starr* reported her position twice daily—8:00 a.m. and 6:00 p.m.—via wireless. The information was in turn broadcast each evening on KFQD, an Anchorage commercial radio station.[32]

The *Starr* was probably the smallest vessel in Alaska Steamship's fleet. And despite the accolades from the Seward paper, the effects of her hard life were apparent. Heavy seas, groundings, an outmoded steam engine, and—though she was overhauled annually in Seattle—probably a lack of comprehensive maintenance took a toll.[33] A seaman who traveled aboard her in the late 1930s described her as "an old boat, dirty and small, and well worn from her years of battling the North Pacific [with] a reek of fuel oil about her, mingled with ancient bilge water."[34] There seemed to also have been long-standing concerns over the safeness of the vessel. This came to a head in

---

d   The *Starr* survived the ordeal and was towed to Seward by the *S.S. Alameda*. It was later towed to Seattle for repairs. In the interim, the 65-foot halibut schooner *Attu* serviced its route.

e   Alonzo Moser, the source of this account, erroneously gave the distance as being about 45 miles.

1938, when the Post Office announced that the *Starr's* contract would not be renewed because it could not comply with "new safety-at-sea regulations."[35] The contract ended June 30, 1938. Because the cost of bringing the vessel up to safety standards was prohibitive, the venerable *Starr* was towed the following year to a ship breaker's yard in Japan for scrapping.[36] She was only 27 years old. During her career on the mail run, the *Starr* graced the cover of *Marine Digest* three times.[37]

As part of his testimony to a congressional committee in 1939, Carlyle Eubanks gave what amounted to a eulogy for the *Starr*: "For 17 years this [vessel's] service was uninterrupted, and although all of us felt that at times the steamer *Starr* was a sore spot, it still gave us all service and was a light upon the ocean when in need; and each month, just as regularly as could be, we knew we could expect our mail and our supplies and have an opportunity to go from one place to another if such were the need."[38]

S.S. *Starr* at a dock in Alaska, probably Chignik or King Cove.

Legislating Mail, Passenger, and Freight Service

Replacing the service provided by the *Starr* proved difficult. The Post Office advertised for bids for a contractor who would furnish a vessel of "sufficient size to handle, in addition to the mails, freight and passenger traffic." It received no response. A second advertisement had the same result. The third time met with some success. Mr. Peter Wold, of Seward, bid approximately $67,000, but his vessel, the *Fern*, was not licensed to carry passengers and had only limited space for freight.[f 39]

The wood-hulled *Fern* was a former lighthouse tender built at Winslow, Washington, in 1915. It had a gross registered tonnage of 207, was 103 feet long, had a beam of 22 feet, and was powered by a 300-horsepower diesel engine.[40] The crew was usually composed of eight men: one master and pilot, one chief mate, three able seamen, one chief engineer, one first assistant engineer, and one second

assistant engineer. When needed, an additional four men were carried to work in the steward's and other departments not connected with the navigation of the vessel.[41]

Wold represented Seward-based Alaska Traders, and wanted to carry the mail as an adjunct to his trading business. He had previously operated the trading vessel *United*, and from a small storehouse on its stern had sold fresh fruit and vegetables and staple groceries. On at least one occasion the vessel's galley served as something of a floating tavern: the wine that was on board for "medicinal purposes" was dispensed to a paying clientele.[42]

The *Fern's* inability to carry passengers or a substantial amount of freight caused great concern among those living in the 28 ports of call along the mail route. Carlyle Eubanks, owner of the Aleutian Livestock Co., effectively made their concerns known to government officials.[43] In June 1939, the House Committee on the Post Office and Post Roads held a hearing titled *Powerboat Service for Alaska*. At the hearing Eubanks explained the need for freight service such as had been rendered by the *Starr*:

The volume of business, the type of so-called "harbors," which in most instances are open ocean water, and a great many other factors do not permit of large freighters calling at the points in question, and we are, therefore, almost entirely dependent upon the service which might be rendered by the boat which is awarded the mail contract.[44]

There was, as well, a definite need for passenger

---

f   The *Fern* was actually owned in equal shares by Wold (Seward), Harold Atentsen (Seattle), and Andrew Anderson (Seattle). Alaska Traders' official address was at Bell Street Dock, Seattle.

Unloading Horses From S.S. Dora, Chignik, Alaska. 176.

Unloading a horse
from the steamer
Dora in Chignik,
circa 1905 1909.

transportation, particularly to Unalaska, where the Bureau of Indian Affairs had established a regional hospital in 1938. Those residing along the mail route found a sympathetic audience in Anthony Dimond, Alaska's nonvoting delegate to Congress. Dimond wanted legislation that would authorize the postmaster general to require that the mail carrier use a "safe and seaworthy boat of sufficient size to carry a reasonable number of passengers and some freight."[45] Soon thereafter, Congress granted Dimond his wish. The Act of August 10, 1939, read:

> *That the Postmaster General may, in his discretion, contract for a period of not exceeding four years, without advertisement therefore, for the carriage of all classes of mail, by steamboat or other powerboat of United States registry, on the route from Seward, by points on Kenai Peninsula, Kodiak Island, Alaska Peninsula, the Aleutian Islands to Umnak Island, and points on Bristol Bay,*

> *Alaska, and vicinity, and back, by a schedule and under the conditions prescribed by the Postmaster General; the contractor to furnish and use in the service a safe and seaworthy boat of sufficient size to provide adequate space for mail, passengers and freight, and annual cost not to exceed $250,000, payment therefore to be made from the appropriation for powerboat service.*[46]

In essence, the mail contract amounted to a subsidy of passenger and freight service along the route. Despite the legislation, the Post Office had no authority to dissolve its contract with Peter Wold. In 1940, however, the *Fern's* Certificate of Inspection was amended to allow it to carry up to 12 passengers.[47] It all became moot when the Japanese attacked Pearl Harbor. The *Fern* was sold to the U.S. Army Corps of Engineers for $40,000.[48] Postwar, the *Fern* was returned to private ownership and, at least for a while, fished king crab in the Bering Sea.[49]

The *Western Trader* carried freight for Ed Kimbrell and Richard Lawrence's Western Trading & Fishing Co.

CHAPTER 3

Mailboats and the Freighters
Western Trader and *Western Pioneer*

Industry Briefs, 1944-1950

THE WAR'S IMPACT

The U.S. military took complete control of all maritime transportation to, from, and within Alaska during World War II. Ships of each of the four major maritime carriers that were operating in Alaska prior to the war (Alaska Steamship, Alaska Transportation, Northland Transportation, and Santa Ana Steamship) were requisitioned by the federal government and operated in theaters around the world under the authority of the War Shipping Administration.

Strategically located along the Pacific Great Circle Route, the Aleutian Islands were on the front line of the U.S. defenses against the Japanese. Major military bases were quickly established at Dutch Harbor and Adak, as well as at Cold Bay, on the Alaska Peninsula. The influx of military personnel caused the population of the Aleutian Islands area to increase from 5,000 to more than 40,000 in the course of a year. The Japanese bombed Dutch Harbor, however, and despite the military's presence, the Japanese were also able to seize and occupy Kiska and Attu Islands.

Though World War II had a profound effect on the Aleutian Islands area, there is no need to repeat here the story that has been so very well chronicled in books such as Brian Garfield's *The Thousand-Mile War* (1969).

At war's end, Alaska was no longer a provincial backwater: World War II had delivered the territory into the 20th century. Military construction projects resulted in a vastly improved infrastructure. New roads, airports, and harbors were constructed, and many of those already in existence were significantly upgraded. Also, a wide array of vessels was constructed for the war effort. No longer needed after the war ended, these vessels were sold (or leased) by the government, often at bargain-basement prices. Many were put into service transporting cargo and in the fishing industry. Some remain in service to this day.

ALASKA STEAMSHIP CO.

Reestablishing adequate maritime transportation was important to the postwar development of Alaska. The effort focused on rebuilding the Seattle-based Alaska Steamship Co. A history of the company is in order.

Alaska Steamship was formed in 1895 and expanded rapidly after the discovery of gold in the Klondike (1897). In 1909, the company was purchased by a group of New York investors known as the Alaska Syndicate, whose primary interest was the development of a body of copper ore at Kennecott, in the Wrangell Mountains. The purchase of the steamship company provided them with an established means to transport their ore. The purchase had a second advantage: efficiency. Except for seasonal loads of canned salmon, Alaska Steamship had previously had little southbound freight. Transporting ore would provide reliable backhaul revenue, bettering the overall economics of the company's operations. Alaska Steamship became far and away the largest carrier in what was termed the "Alaska trade," and for many years enjoyed a near monopoly position.

Mining ended at Kennecott in 1938, and the business began to languish. In the years just prior to World War II, Alaska Steamship was operating 17 vessels, supplemented seasonally by two to six additional ships. During the war, the company's entire fleet was requisitioned by the government.

The S.S. *Alaska*, circa 1920, was typical of the Alaska Steamship Co. fleet in the pre-World War II years, combining elegance with functionality and carrying both passengers and freight.

As a result of war casualties, sale due to obsolescence and heavy war usage, and transfer under the Lend-Lease program, Alaska Steamship's fleet had dwindled to five vessels.[1] Despite the losses, some said that operators in the Alaska trade had been "bailed out by the war."[2] Indeed, in an attempt to rebuild freight capacity to Alaska, the government leased surplus freighters at the nominal rate of one dollar per year as well as assuming the cost of hull and marine insurance on these vessels.[3]

Apparently seeing some future in the trade, the Skinner & Eddy Corp., of Seattle, purchased the Alaska Steamship Co. in 1944.[4] Alaska Steamship became the largest of the Seattle-owned steamship lines and what *Marine Digest* called the "bench mark of the city's trade with the 49th state."[5] *Marine Digest* missed no opportunity to lavish praise on Alaska Steamship. Alaskans, on the other hand, resented the control that Alaska Steamship had over their lives. Territorial Governor Ernest Gruening was particularly vehement, stating that the company was a "seaway robber."[6]

Tom Pelly, Seattle's representative in Congress, dismissed Gruening as "a professional enemy of both Seattle and the Alaska Steamship Co."[7]

PRIBILOF ISLANDS

The war was particularly hard on the people of the Pribilof Islands. The government considered the islands vulnerable to attack, and their inhabitants were forcibly relocated to Southeast Alaska in 1942, though a sealing crew did return for the harvest in 1943.[8] At war's end, the people of the Pribilofs were moved back to their islands. Transportation to and from the Pribilofs in the first five years after the war was provided by a combination of military ships and the *Penguin*, the latter of which was being operated by the U.S. Fish and Wildlife Service, the successor to the Bureau of Fisheries. Military ships involved in the supply effort were the *Morlin*, *Achernar*, *Thurban*, *Titania*, and *Andromeda*.

In 1950, after making two trips to the Pribilofs, the

Penguin was seriously damaged by a fire while at her moorings in Seattle. She was quickly replaced by the 148-foot *Penguin II*, formerly the *FS-246* and *Lt. Raymond Zussman*.[a] This steel vessel had the capacity for some 350 tons of cargo, about twice that of her predecessor.[9] The *Penguin II* continued to serve the Pribilof Islands until 1963; she broke down that year and was quickly replaced by the *FSR-791*, a 205-foot reefer ship that had been in lay-up on the East Coast.[b] After one trip, the vessel was brought back to Seattle and fitted out for Bering Sea conditions. She was renamed *Pribilof*.[10] With a crew of 18 or 19, a capacity of 1,000 tons of cargo, and a cruising speed of 11 knots, the *Pribilof* would service her namesake islands for nearly two more decades.[11]

CARGO MANIFEST LAW EXCLUSION

There was good news in the spring of 1948 for all engaged in the Alaska and Hawaii trade. President Truman signed legislation that exempted the two territories from the Cargo Manifest Law, the 1902 legislation that required export declarations on merchandise shipped to the territories.[12] The Cargo Manifest Law was designed to give the government an idea of the flow of commerce between the United States and its territories. The reason for the exemption was that the information being collected was incomplete because a significant portion of the merchandise coming into Alaska and Hawaii was from mail order catalog businesses such as Montgomery Ward and Sears. It was mostly shipped by mail, which required no customs declaration.

POSTWAR FISHERY DEVELOPMENT IN THE BERING SEA

Two postwar developments in the Bering Sea area helped to shape the area's economy of today.

The first was the development of the king crab industry. Lowell Wakefield, the acknowledged pioneer of the industry, began his efforts to catch, process, and market Alaska king crab in 1946 aboard his custom-built factory trawler *Deep*

The U.S. Fish and Wildlife Service's *Penguin II* discharging cargo to a lighter at St. Paul Island in July of 1952.

Sea.[c] It wasn't easy going at first. In 1947, Wakefield reported to his business partners, "We have caught fewer crabs and fish, produced less crab meat and fillets, sold our product more slowly, and spent money more quickly than we ever anticipated."[13] But Wakefield persisted, and his operation became a viable concern in 1950, ushering in a boom the likes of which Alaska fishermen had never seen. Wakefield not only pioneered the king crab fishery, he also pioneered the practice of transferring his product to small refrigerated freighters so that his vessels could remain on the grounds.[d] [14]

The second development was the virtual invasion by Japanese fishermen of the eastern Bering Sea. The Japanese had been fishing in the eastern Bering Sea since 1930, but not with the intensity they showed in the postwar years.[15] This effort began modestly in 1954, but by 1960 the Japanese were harvesting nearly a half million metric tons of fish.[e] And their catch continued to grow: in 1972, the Japanese catch was nearly two million tons. Nearly a half million tons more

a The military designation "FS" indicates "freighter, small."

b The military designation "FSR" indicates "freighter, small, refrigerated."

c In the early years of the fishery, king crab were caught in otter trawls. Wakefield's operation also processed incidentally caught groundfish.

d The product was delivered to Bellingham Cold Storage (Bellingham, Wash.) for additional processing.

e Fisheries managers use metric tons as the standard for measuring the groundfish catch in the Bering Sea.

Aleutian Mail in
Juneau, Alaska, 1947.

were caught that year by the U.S.S.R. fleet.[16] Few believed the harvest was sustainable. Adding insult to injury, some of the fishing activity was visible from U.S. shores. This aroused a host of sentiments—protectionist, conservationist, industrialist—in the United States that ultimately led to legislation in 1976 that unilaterally extended the U.S. maritime boundary to 200 miles from its coasts. The subsequent "Americanization" of the fisheries within the 200-mile limit resulted in the development of a vast industrial enterprise that soon stretched from Akutan to Adak and to the Pribilof Islands and beyond. Today, transporting the goods and materials that sustain this enterprise, and moving the final product to market, involves the full range of transport vessels. Small freighters, tramp freighters, huge container ships, and tugboats pulling barges loaded with containers all have an important part in the effort. But it was the small freighters, such as those that carried the mail, that were the pioneers in the trade.

The Mailboats

The first postwar vessel on the Aleutian mail run was the *Clarinda*. The vessel was about 110 feet long, and could carry 14 passengers plus 70 tons of mail and freight. Her first and only trip departed Seward in early January 1947.

The *Clarinda* was experiencing engine problems and leaking oil as she entered Squaw Harbor, but it was decided to push on to Sand Point (about 10 miles from Squaw Harbor) to fix the problems. On January 12, not long after tying to a dock at Sand Point, there was an explosion aboard the *Clarinda*. The vessel immediately caught fire, and the dock was partly destroyed before she could be towed away. The *Clarinda* was beyond saving, and she was towed to deep water, where she sank. Fortunately, there were no fatalities in the *Clarinda's* demise, although one crewmember was injured. Several sacks of mail later washed ashore.[17]

The 136-foot former U.S. Navy minesweeper *Aleutian Mail* then took up the run. The vessel was constructed in 1944, was rated at 263 gross tons, had a beam of 26 feet, and was powered by a pair of 500-horsepower General Motors diesel engines. She could carry 200 tons of mail and freight in three unrefrigerated holds.[18] The vessel's crew sold various items, including meat, eggs, vegetables, cigarettes, and even Christmas trees.

The *Aleutian Mail*, owned and operated by Captain J. H. Petrich, carried the mail for a little less than a year. This short period was capped by a series of unfortunate incidents, two of which cost people their lives. The first was in December 1947, when a crewmember drowned after the skiff in which he was attempting to land the mail at Cape Sarichef (Unimak Island) capsized. The following month, the *Aleutian Mail* ran aground in Pavlof Bay, perhaps due to a problem with the vessel's radar. At the next high tide, Captain Petrich managed to maneuver the vessel off the beach and into deep water a half mile out, where he dropped two anchors. The vessel's rudder and propellers were too severely damaged to allow further travel, so the Coast Guard's *Cedar*, a converted lighthouse tender that was in the vicinity, towed her to Sand Point. There she was anchored out to await a tow to Seattle. Two days later four crewmen perished in a skiff accident, apparently while traveling between the *Aleutian Mail* and the Sand Point dock. The *Aleutian Mail* was eventually towed to Kodiak and then to Seattle. Her contract with the Post Office was later annulled.[19]

In February 1948, the 109-foot *Lois Anderson*, a lumbering wood-hulled power scow built for the Army during WWII, took over the run. She quit after making only one trip, and was not immediately replaced because the Post Office could find no suitable bidders who were willing to operate under the established price ceiling. As an interim solution, Reeve Airways was contracted to fly the mail from Anchorage to Cold Bay, Unalaska, and Atka.[20] The 65-foot vessel *Moby Dick* was contracted to deliver mail between Cold Bay and ports along the way to Scotch Cap in the west and Chignik in the east. Service was thrice monthly from April through September and twice monthly during the rest of the year.[21] Unfortunately, Reeve Airways provided little, if any, passenger and freight service. This led to complaints by residents whose existence in this remote part of Alaska was essentially dependent on the service that mailboats had traditionally provided.

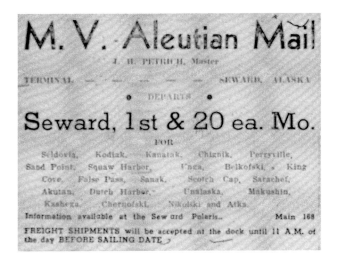

GARLAND

Mailboat service along the route was reinstated in late April 1949 with the vessel *Garland*.[22] Her master was Captain R. Jacobson, who had previously served on the *Fern*. The wood-hulled *Garland* (ex *FS-248*) was constructed in Bellingham, Washington, in 1944. At 544 gross registered tons, she was the largest and, according to the *Seward Seaport Record*, the finest vessel to ever make the mail run. The *Garland* was 139 feet long, with a beam of 33 feet and a draft of 14 feet, and was powered by a single 875-horsepower Fairbanks-Morse diesel engine.[23] Her actual cargo capacity was 350 to 400 tons general and 50 tons refrigerated, and she was licensed to carry 12 passengers in international waters and 16 in Alaska waters. The *Garland* was owned by the Berger Transportation Co., of Seattle, and prior to being used on the mail route she had been chartered by the Aleutian Islands Navigation Co. to haul cargo from Seattle to Alaska. The vessel had apparently made only two trips before a labor dispute ended that venture.[f][24]

As a mailboat, the *Garland* operated on a year-round monthly Seattle-Seward-Nikolski-Seattle route, with the mail

---

f   Heinie Berger, the owner of Berger Transportation, was originally based in Kasilof, Alaska, on Cook Inlet. He purchased his first freight vessel with winnings from the Nenana Ice Classic, a pool in which contestants guess the time the ice will break up on the Tanana River, near Fairbanks, Alaska. Prior to World War II, Berger operated two vessels, the *Discoverer* and probably the *Kasilof*, between Seward and ports on Cook Inlet. The *Discoverer* sometimes transported passengers and freight between Seattle and Seward.

being picked up at Seward and delivered to 25 individual locations, some of which were visited on both the outbound and inbound legs of the trip.[25] The mail contract called for payment of approximately $156,000 per year in 1949, and approximately $233,000 in 1954.[26] The approximate annual operating costs for the vessel were reported in the spring of 1954 as being $150,000 for officers and crew, $30,000 for longshoring, $36,000 for provisions and supplies, $35,000 for fuel, and $20,000 for repairs in shipyards.[27] The *Garland* provided considerable service to the sheep industry on Umnak Island, annually transporting about 1,000 bags of wool to Seattle, and occasionally transporting sheep and cattle to the island.[28]

In September 1950, the *Garland* struck some rocks and went to Seattle for repairs. The vessel *Pomare* operated in her stead until the *Garland* returned to service in January 1951.[29] In the fall of 1951, Captain Edward Kimbrell became master of the *Garland*. Richard Lawrence was his chief mate. Together these two men would figure very prominently in the development of the Aleutian trade as we know it today.

Kimbrell was born in 1917, and he first went to sea at age 14. With the Dollar Line, he had sailed the world's oceans. From 1936 through 1939, Kimbrell attended the University of Washington, and during the years 1941 to 1946, he sailed as mate, master, and pilot for Alaska Steamship Co. In the years prior to shipping out on the *Garland*, Kimbrell was the agent for the Masters, Mates and Pilots Association.

Lawrence was the same age as Kimbrell. He had a chief mate's license and an Alaska pilot's license, and he had sailed as chief mate with the Alaska Steamship Co.[30] For a while, he was a member of the so-called "Mahoney Gang," a radical labor group that tried to control Seattle's waterfront.[31]

Anna Martin described a pleasant voyage on the *Garland* under Kimbrell and Lawrence in her book *Around and About Alaska*. In July 1952, the adventurous woman on holiday traveled from Seward to Unalaska and back on the *Garland*. She recalled it as a "trim, businesslike vessel" with a crew of 15. Deck freight on the trip included a pedigree bull (Gorgeous George) in a none-too-large crate, and several crates of chickens. The vessel made about 20 stops on its way to Unalaska. At only about half the stops was there a dock. At dockless locations, a small motorboat was lowered and

the captain and first mate, often wearing hip boots, took the mail and supplies to shore. Like the *Fern*, the *Garland* was something of a floating store. Its inventory was limited to potatoes, onions, ice cream, and comic books. Martin made no mention of liquor on the vessel.[32]

In July 1954, Berger Transportation Co. lost the mail contract. The regional operations director for the Postal Service apparently considered the *Garland* operation unsatisfactory, but would not say why.[33] Ed Kimbrell and Richard Lawrence were out of work, but they would soon use their knowledge of the Aleutian trade to establish a cargo operation of their own.

CAPTAIN NIELS THOMSEN'S *EXPANSION*

The Seward-Nikolski mail contract was awarded to the Aleutian Marine Transportation Co., which was owned by Captain Niels Thomsen, a former U.S. Coast Guard commander.[34] Aleutian Marine Transportation operated the vessel *Expansion* (ex *FS-37*) on the route. The wood-hulled vessel was constructed at Northwestern Shipbuilding, in Bellingham, Washington, the same yard that had built the *Garland*. At 107 feet in length, the *Expansion* was somewhat smaller than the *Garland*. She had a beam of 27 feet and a draft of 12 feet, and was registered at 270 gross tons. The vessel was powered by a pair of 320-horsepower Atlas Imperial diesel engines that pushed her along at a speed of 10 knots. Freight capacity was 110 tons of dry cargo and a limited amount of deck cargo. As well, there were two "large reefer boxes" for frozen cargo. It seems that some hold space was later refrigerated to bring frozen capacity to 10 tons. The *Expansion* was manned by a crew of 14 men and could transport up to 16 passengers.

The first voyage of the *Expansion* along the mail route was in August 1954. She was under the command of Captain John Pym, a former master of the *Garland*.[35] Thomsen took over operation of the vessel not long afterward.

Thomsen did business as the Aleutian Marine Transport Co., and in 1955, he advertised that his vessel—which was also a floating wholesale and retail store—departed Seward the first week of every month and served Port Graham, Seldovia, Kodiak, Chignik, Perryville, Sand Point, Squaw Harbor,

Mailboat *Expansion* delivering monthly mail to False Pass in the early 1960s. Bill Bright (center) was the community's postmaster. Bright later became superintendent of the local salmon cannery.

The *Expansion* docked in the Lake Washington Ship Canal circa 1962.

Unga, Belkofski, King Cove, Cold Bay, Pauloff Harbor, Sanak, Ikatan, False Pass, Akutan, Unalaska, Kashega, Chernofski, and Nikolski.[36]

For the communities along its route, the mailboat was a primary vehicle for disseminating regional news. In June 1956, Niels Thomsen formalized this service: he began a newspaper, the *Mailboat Monitor*. His stated goal was to foster "knowledge and understanding" among the communities he served. The paper designated a local individual in each community, collectively known as The Chain Gang, to report the news. There was as well a special column, "Aleutian Solutions," to provide advice to the lovelorn. The first editions of the intermittent newspaper were published in Seward. Later editions were published in Kodiak. The paper was printed by the *Anchorage Daily News*.

The enterprising Thomsen was also an agent of the Bank of Kodiak and at one point offered to make the *Expansion* into something of a floating bookmobile that would deposit boxes of donated books along the route. There seems to be no record as to whether the book venture was ever brought to fruition.

The following is an account of the *Expansion* at Nikolski, on Umnak Island, in 1957:

> When the "MV Expansion" came in, we learned what the natives meant by Christmas twelve times a year. . . . At Nikolski she anchors beyond the reef, and every man in the village helps load the wool and unload the supplies she brings for stores and individuals. Everyone sighs with relief when the work is finished, then tears into the letters, magazines and packages from Sears and Wards.[37]

WESTERN TRADER

As a result of the experience gained with Alaska Steamship and on the *Garland*, Ed Kimbrell and Richard Lawrence were acutely aware of transportation issues peculiar to western Alaska. The two recognized an opportunity to transport freight directly between Seattle and the Aleutian Islands area.

In 1955, Kimbrell and Lawrence formed the Western Trading & Fishing Co. and acquired the 120-foot steel-hulled vessel *Western Trader* from the Washington Fish & Oyster Co.[g] The vessel had been utilized primarily to service Washington Fish & Oyster's cannery at Port William (Shuyak Island), Alaska.[38]

Kimbrell and Lawrence's plan was to develop a freight service to transport dry and frozen cargo for fish-processing operations in western Alaska. With the *Western Trader* they would include service to small ports that Alaska Steamship, with its relatively large and expensive-to-operate freighters, could not economically provide. One fish processor at about that time claimed that Alaska Steamship would not go into a port without a minimum of 100 tons of cargo.[39] Alaska Steamship had plenty of capacity to carry frozen seafood. Since 1948 the company had been operating the refrigerated vessels *Lucidor* and *Palisana* to transport frozen cargo from Seattle to Alaska under contract with the U.S. Army. Included in the vessels' southbound cargo was a considerable amount of frozen seafood. Since some of the ports served under the Army contract were in the Aleutian Islands and on the Alaska Peninsula, it is likely that some of the frozen seafood transported south came from this area. The Army contract was canceled in 1954, but—to the great relief of seafood processors—Alaska Steamship kept both vessels in service into the latter half of 1956.[40]

An advantage of Kimbrell and Lawrence's plan to serve the Aleutian Islands area was that the king crab fishery was at that time year-round. In contrast to Alaska's salmon fisheries, there would be no down time. A drawback of their operation was that the *Western Trader* was relatively small, particularly when considering the expanse of often perilous waters that she would have to negotiate. It was with this modest vessel, however, that Kimbrell and Lawrence boldly pioneered what grew to be known as the Aleutian trade, providing regular freight service directly from Puget Sound ports to the geographic region that encompasses the Aleutian and Pribilof Islands and the lower Alaska Peninsula.

The *Western Trader* had a beam of 24 feet and was powered by twin 220-horsepower Atlas diesel engines. She had been constructed in California in 1920 as the *Casco*. At some

---

g   The 1958 Record of the American Bureau of Shipping shows the *Western Trader* as being owned by L.B.K, Inc. If one assumes that the L stands for Lawrence and the K for Kimbrell, the B may stand for (R. R.) Bivins, an early partner in the *Western Pioneer*.

point, she was taken to Hawaii, renamed *Kailua*, and operated in the inter-island freight service. Around 1933, she was purchased and brought to Puget Sound by Captain Harry Crosby. Crosby used her in connection with a cannery venture at Chignik, Alaska, and then sold her to Wallace Bailey of the Western Shipping Co. The *Kailua* was renamed *Western Trader* and, in preparation for service between Puget Sound and Alaska, was repowered and extensively rebuilt, including refrigerating the cargo space to enable the transport of frozen product.[41]

World War II changed everything. The *Western Trader* was acquired by the Navy early in 1942. Initially designated *YAG-11*, she was renamed *Baranof* and deployed to Alaska, where she shuttled passengers and freight between ports that included Ketchikan, Sitka, Kodiak, and Sand Point.[h] She was decommissioned in 1944, and purchased by Washington Fish & Oyster in 1947.[42] In the fall of 1948, known again as the *Western Trader*, she discharged a cargo of fresh meat and produce in Seward.[43]

Kimbrell and Lawrence, described by *Marine Digest* as a "hardworking pair," operated the *Western Trader* for, at best, three years.[44] Theirs does not appear to have been a scheduled operation. A former manager at Washington Fish & Oyster (now Ocean Beauty Seafoods) recalled that cargoes were solicited by an agent. Washington Fish & Oyster found it less expensive to pay Kimbrell and Lawrence to haul their cargo than to operate the *Western Trader* themselves.[45] The *Western Trader*, however, was sold back to Washington Fish & Oyster after Kimbrell and Lawrence decided to purchase a larger vessel.[i] [46]

WESTERN PIONEER, RUGGED STALWART OF THE ALEUTIAN TRADE

Recognizing the need for a larger vessel, Kimbrell and Lawrence with R. R. Bivins, part owner and general manager of Seattle Shipbuilding and Drydocking Company, purchased the 183-foot wood-hulled vessel *Vent* on Christmas Eve, 1956.[47] The *Vent* (formerly *ARS-29*) was a rescue and salvage ship constructed for the U.S. Navy at the Bellingham Marine Railway Co., in Bellingham, Washington.[j] She and her four sister ships may have been the largest wood-hulled vessels constructed for the military during World War II. The *Vent* was commissioned in 1944 and decommissioned two years later. Kimbrell and Lawrence's attorney several years later claimed that the *Vent* was "practically a new ship" when his clients had acquired her. He also suggested that since she was the last-built of her class, she was "likely the best." Kimbrell and Lawrence, he said, had purchased the vessel in the belief that she was of ideal design for use in the Aleutian Islands: "comfortable and safe, of sufficient size for rough going, and still fast enough to maintain her schedule."[48] Time would show the *Vent*, rechristened *Western Pioneer*, to be an extremely rugged and seaworthy vessel that was very well suited to her trade.

The *Western Pioneer* had a beam of 37 feet and a draft of 15 feet. She was registered at 1,042 gross tons, and powered by a diesel-electric system comprised of four 450-horsepower Cooper-Bessemer diesel engines driving two electric propulsion motors.[49] Her service speed was 12 to 13 knots, and she carried 40,000 gallons of fuel, which was pretty much consumed in one round-trip voyage from Puget Sound to the Aleutian Islands area.[50]

In August 1957, the Kimbrell-Lawrence Transportation Co. was organized to take ownership of the *Western Pioneer*. The firm obtained a Small Business Administration loan of $175,000, which was used to renovate the vessel and convert her into a refrigerator ship. The work was completed in August 1958.[51] Kimbrell-Lawrence Transportation's Seattle terminal was located on the Lake Washington Ship Canal.[52]

That fall, Ed Kimbrell explained to the Federal Maritime Board—the federal agency then responsible for the regulation of shipping—his firm's intent to operate the *Western Pioneer* as a tramp freighter: "Our vessel has not carried passengers, we have no scheduled operations or regular route or designated ports of call, and we have no plans for operating as a common carrier." Voyages would be made, said Kimbrell, "at such times as our vessel is engaged by prospective shippers."[53] The *Western Pioneer* operated under a contract with the

---

h   The military designation YAG indicates a "miscellaneous auxiliary service craft."

i   In 1960, Washington Fish & Oyster sold the *Western Trader* to a group of individuals who intended to establish a colony in the Galapagos Islands. The much-publicized venture was short-lived.

---

j   The military designation ARS indicates a "diver class rescue and salvage ship."

Sailors' Union of the Pacific, and carried a crew of 13 men.[54]

The first voyage of the *Western Pioneer* was in October 1958. Her cargo was refrigerated stores for Shemya, in the Aleutian Islands, which was an intermediate stop for Northwest Orient Airlines on its recently inaugurated trans-Pacific flights.[55] The business developed rapidly and, as originally intended, mainly revolved around servicing the fishing industry.

It was about this time that D. E. Skinner, president of Alaska Steamship, complained that his company had lost 90 percent of its Alaska-to-Puget-Sound frozen seafood business to small freighters.[56] This was despite the fact that Alaska Steamship had begun modifying its vessels to carry refrigerated vans on deck to augment below-deck frozen storage capacity.[k][57] Seafood processors gave two reasons why they preferred the small freighters:

Efficiency. Small freighters could deliver product directly to seafood company docks in Puget Sound, eliminating the need for loading product on trucks, then unloading it.[58]

Flexibility. Small freighters offered frequent service, were willing to take fish boxed or loose, and would arrange cooperative charters among several seafood processors.[59]

Alaska seafood processed by freezing at that time consisted mostly of halibut and king crab.

Captain Kimbrell and his crew's prowess and bravery were shown in the rescue of eight Canadian fishermen on Unimak Island on August 26, 1959. Kimbrell intercepted a distress call from the 73-foot halibut boat *Queen Kathleen*, which had grounded in heavy weather off Cape Lutke, west of Unimak Pass. The *Western Pioneer* immediately raced to assist, but had to proceed dangerously close to the rocky shore to locate the stranded vessel. Shortly after the *Queen Kathleen* was sighted, she began to break up. Fortunately, the crew had made it to shore, but was stranded on a rocky, storm-lashed beach. *Marine Digest* printed an account of the rescue: "The *Western Pioneer* maneuvered in close and lowered a life boat which rowed ashore towing a surf line from the ship. The boat was carried onto a small sandy beach in a cleft in

the rocks by a wave; the survivors jumped in and the boat was hauled off when the next wave struck. In this manner, the entire crew of eight was rescued without injury."[60]

For his part in the rescue, Kimbrell received a letter of commendation from the Commandant of the U.S. Coast Guard. In the commendation, Vice Admiral Alfred Richmond wrote: "The prompt and effective response of the *Western Pioneer* in this emergency reflects the highest credit on the state of readiness of her officers and crew under your command."[61] More honors were forthcoming. In June 1961, Kimbrell and each of his crewmembers were awarded meritorious service medals by the U.S. Maritime Administration, which also designated the *Western Pioneer* as a Gallant Ship.[l][62] The designation cited the "courage,

U.S.S. *Baranof* in 1942. The Navy decommissioned her in 1944, and she was purchased by the Washington Fish & Oyster Co. and renamed *Western Trader*. Ed Kimbrell and Richard Lawrence acquired her in 1955 to haul cargo between Seattle and Alaska.

l   The Gallant Ship Award was authorized in 1944 by executive order of President Franklin Roosevelt. Under the order as codified today, "The Secretary of Transportation may issue a Gallant Ship Award and a citation to a United States vessel or to a foreign-flag vessel participating in outstanding or gallant action in marine disasters or other emergencies for the purpose of saving life or property at sea."

k   Alaska Steamship was a pioneer in containerized transportation.

U.S. Navy Diver Class rescue and salvage ship *ARS-29 Vent* was built at Bellingham, Washington, during World War II. She was decommissioned after the war, and in 1958 entered the Aleutian trade as the *Western Pioneer.*

resourcefulness, expert seamanship and teamwork of her master, officers and crew" exhibited in the rescue of the crew of the *Queen Kathleen.*[63] This was only the third time since the end of World War II that the Gallant Ship Award had been made. The previous recipient, the 455-foot freighter *Meredith Victory*, rescued some 14,000 South Korean villagers who were in imminent peril of being overrun by enemy forces during the Korean War.[64]

LAST YEARS OF THE SEWARD-NIKOLSKI MAIL CONTRACT

Around 1958, the inhabitants along the Seward-Nikolski mail route were voicing complaints that they were not entirely satisfied with the service provided by Captain Thomsen's *Expansion.*[65] A major complaint was that the *Expansion* received freight for the Aleutian Islands area at Kodiak, adding more transportation and longshoring costs in comparison to a direct shipment from Seattle. They also thought that service would be improved if the mail contract were put out to competitive bid instead of having a Post Office official choose the contractor. Alaska became a state on January 3, 1959, and the first regular session of its legislature addressed the issue in a memorial—an official statement of desire—that urged simply that "the contract for the transportation of surface mail between Seward and Nikolski be opened to competitive bidding."[66] Thomsen maintained that the whole issue revolved around Seattle interests who wanted to combine the mail service with other operations.[67] He was likely referring to Ed Kimbrell and Richard Lawrence. At any rate, the Post Office responded positively to the legislature's request and in May advertised for bids for the Seward-Nikolski mailboat run for a two-year period beginning September 1, 1959.[68] Four bids were received. Thomsen's was accepted.[69]

Despite Kimbrell's assertion, it seems that he and his partner had not entirely dismissed the idea of operating as a common carrier. Though their business was beginning to flourish, they continued to work to obtain the mail contract to the Aleutian Islands area.

Their efforts were frowned upon by Alaska's delegation to Congress. In 1959, Sen. E. L. Bartlett introduced a bill (hearing held on July 8, 1959) to amend the 1939 mailboat legislation by adding that the contracting vessel "shall be operated exclusively on the [Seward-Nikolski] route described in the [1939] Act."[70] An identical bill was introduced by Ralph Rivers, Alaska's lone representative in the House. The proposed amendment would have precluded a Seattle-to-Alaska operator from obtaining a contract for mail service from Seward to the Aleutian Islands area. The rationale was that an operator using the subsidized mail contract as an adjunct to a Seattle-to-Alaska freight business would have an undue advantage over unsubsidized operators on the same run.[71] The bill passed in the U.S. Senate, but did not fare well in the House.

A hearing was held on the issue on May 6, 1960, in front of the House Committee on Post Office and Civil Service. To represent their interests and speak for them, Kimbrell and Lawrence retained an attorney, Raymond Peterson.

According to Peterson, Kimbrell and Lawrence had purchased the *Western Pioneer* specifically to obtain a mail contract to the Aleutian Islands area. He insisted that the *Western Pioneer* could consistently make the monthly Seattle-Seward-Nikolski-Seattle run in 23 days "without any difficulty," pointing out that the slower *Garland* had once made the trip in 21 days. The people in the Aleutian Islands area favored this sort of service.

Despite the failure of the proposed legislation to become law, Kimbrell and Lawrence never obtained the mail contract. In 1961, however, Thomsen substantially upgraded and modified his operation to accommodate the need for direct freight service from Seattle.

Thomsen purchased the 150-foot vessel *Dennis Winn*, which was formerly operated by the U.S. Fish and Wildlife Service. The cost of the vessel was reportedly $60,000, and Thomsen spent an additional $100,000 renovating her to carry freight and passengers. When completed, the vessel could accommodate 16 passengers and had a freight capacity of 450 tons, 75 of which was refrigerated. Additional space was refrigerated late that summer. The vessel was renamed the *Expansion*, and the original *Expansion* was put up for sale. The *Expansion* (2) could travel at a speed of 11.5 knots, significantly faster than its predecessor's 10 knots. With the new vessel, Thomsen maintained his monthly sailings from Seward and inaugurated every-other-month service from Seattle (Ames Terminal) to Aleutian Islands area ports via Ketchikan and Seward. With the Seattle departures, Thomsen expected a 30 to 40 percent reduction in freight costs as compared to picking up cargo in Kodiak. Also, his was the first passenger vessel service to Alaska since 1954, when Alaska Steamship ceased carrying passengers.[72]

Thomsen's mail contract was set to expire on June 30, 1963. Though *Marine Digest* had reported in early 1962 that the Post Office had no plans to terminate the service, something had changed.[73] In the fall of 1963, Thomsen's Aleutian Marine Transport advertised a different service with a different vessel. The mail route was now a Kodiak to Nikolski run, and the vessel employed was the *Fairbanks*, which connected with Alaska Steamship at the city dock in Kodiak.[74] According to Thomsen, the Post Office discontinued the mailboat service in 1964.[75] From that point on, the Post Office began contracting with airlines to carry the mail.

Thomsen may have been done delivering the mail to the Aleutians, but he was not done with the Aleutians. He had watched the king crab industry develop and was among the first to recognize the opportunity to process the big crustaceans at Dutch Harbor. In 1964, the same year his mail contract ended, he founded Aleutian King Crab and began processing crab on the *Bethel I*, a former minesweeper hull that he kept moored to a dock at Dutch Harbor.[76] King crab was viewed as an economical alternative to lobster, and domestic consumption was soaring. Thomsen's production was transported to Puget Sound mostly by the *Western Pioneer*.

Western Pioneer at Bellingham Cold Storage dock circa 1964. Frozen crab from Alaska was reprocessed at Bellingham Cold Storage.

CHAPTER 4

Kimbrell-Lawrence Transportation: "Ship West with the Best"

KIMBRELL AND LAWRENCE'S BUSINESS CONTINUED TO GROW. In 1960, *Marine Digest* reported that the *Western Pioneer* was departing Seattle fully loaded approximately every 18 days. To accommodate the growth of their business, the Kimbrell-Lawrence Transportation Co. moved to a larger facility at Pier 50. Atop their warehouse was a sign reading "Pioneer Alaska Docks." Kimbrell and Lawrence's routine while in Seattle was for Kimbrell to call on customers and solicit cargo while Lawrence oversaw the unloading and loading of their vessel.[a] Once the *Western Pioneer* was ready to go, Kimbrell would come aboard and, with Lawrence as first mate, cast off for Alaska.[1]

There was talk as well of expansion involving the acquisition of one or more additional vessels.[2] Her owners considered the *Western Pioneer* to be ideally suited to her trade, and tried in vain to locate and purchase a sister ship. There were none to be had that were not under foreign registry.[3] Under a provision of the Merchant Marine Act of 1920 (Jones Act), a U.S.-built/U.S.-flagged vessel that came under foreign registry lost its right to engage in the U.S. coastwise trade.[4] Kimbrell and Lawrence also attempted to purchase the *Pribilof* from the U.S. government, but were unsuccessful.[5]

As well as serving the fishing industry, the *Western Pioneer* carried freight for the U.S. military. A shipment from the Naval Supply Depot in Seattle destined for U.S. Air Force Distant Early Warning (DEW-Line) stations in 1961 consisted of 325 tons of frozen cargo and 175 tons of chilled cargo.[6]

To help keep up with the demand for refrigerated space, in 1962 the stern of the *Western Pioneer* was enclosed and fitted with refrigeration. This gave the vessel a total of 40,000 cubic feet of cargo space, all refrigerated.[7] The vessel could carry about 1.6 million pounds of frozen crab meat, or 1.2 million pounds of frozen halibut. Crab meat was shipped in cases containing four 15-pound blocks. A capacity load of halibut would equal about 30,000 individual fish stacked in the holds like cordwood.[8]

The year 1963 started out with a mishap. As the *Western Pioneer* was slowly maneuvering up to the Ballard Dock in Seattle, Kimbrell signaled the engine room for "full astern." The signal was either misinterpreted or had been sent wrong, because the engineer put the vessel in "full forward." The *Western Pioneer* smashed into a float and struck three vessels. One vessel sank and the other two were damaged, one beyond repair.[9]

By that year, Kimbrell-Lawrence Transportation had moved its Seattle operations to Pier 66, a unionized (International Longshore and Warehouse Union) dock. In the fall of 1963, the firm began operating a scheduled service in addition to its usual charter service. It also began advertising in *Marine Digest* with the slogan "Ship West with the Best." *Marine Digest* noted that Kimbrell and Lawrence didn't bother with the protected Inside Passage, but took the most direct open-sea route between Cape Flattery (the entrance to Puget Sound) and Kodiak. The duration of round-trip voyages to the Aleutian Islands area at that time usually ranged from 16 to 23 days, depending on the weather, the number of ports visited, and the time spent in ports.[10] Voyages tended to get longer as the business grew.

---

a   On one occasion, a load of steel pipe that was being carried on the stern deck of the *Western Pioneer* began coming apart in heavy seas in the Gulf of Alaska. Kimbrell and Lawrence secured it by welding the pipe together.

By 1964, the *Western Pioneer* began regularly servicing the Pribilof Islands on its August and September voyages. The southbound cargo from the Pribilofs on each voyage consisted of 300 tons of combined ground seal carcasses—"sealburger"—(a frozen product packed in 50-pound bags) and seal skins (packed in wooden boxes that often weighed more than 100 pounds). The sealburger was destined for mink farms in Oregon, the skins for a furrier in St. Louis. There were no docks at either St. Paul or St. George Island on which to unload and load, so the traditional baidars, now powered with outboard motors, lightered the cargo from the shore.[11] On one trip to the Pribilofs in 1963, the *Western Pioneer*'s cargo included four dump trucks. To get them to shore, each truck was stripped down as much as possible and lowered onto a platform rigged atop four lashed-together baidars.[12]

In 1964, Kimbrell-Lawrence Transportation served Kodiak and provided the only year-round service to 17 outports in Southwest Alaska. In its 10 voyages that year, the *Western Pioneer* carried about 5 percent of the total cargo transported to and from the area. Alaska Steamship, by contrast, carried about 92 percent, much of which was to supply the U.S. Navy base at Adak. The total amount carried by Kimbrell-Lawrence Transportation was 10,376 tons (4,477 tons northbound and 5,899 southbound).[13] On a per-voyage basis during the late 1960s, the *Western Pioneer*'s gross revenue was typically $60-75 thousand for northbound cargo and $20-25 thousand for southbound.[14]

In about 1965, the routine at Kimbrell-Lawrence changed. Paul Odsen was hired to run the *Western Pioneer*, which allowed Ed Kimbrell to focus on soliciting cargo and maintaining customer relations while Richard Lawrence handled port operations. The company strove to maintain a monthly schedule, and to have the *Western Pioneer* depart on Fridays (a dangerous move, to superstitious mariners), which gave customers most of the workweek to deliver cargo. A crew under Richard Lawrence would usually begin loading cargo on Tuesdays. Once the vessel departed Seattle, except for an occasional phone call from Dutch Harbor or Sand Point, the *Western Pioneer* was pretty much out of contact for the 22-to-25-day duration of a typical voyage. First word of her return was usually received through Bellingham

Cold Storage, which was the destination of frozen crab transported by Kimbrell-Lawrence.[b] Paul Odsen often got off at Bellingham, and after the ship's cargo was unloaded, Ed Kimbrell and Dick Lawrence brought the *Western Pioneer* to Seattle. This arrangement allowed Odsen some additional time with his family. In Seattle, the *Western Pioneer* was refueled (diesel fuel at that time cost about 8.5 cents per gallon) and its machinery gone over by mechanics from a local shipyard. The vessel's engines, in particular, required a lot of attention, and the repair bill after a single voyage could be as much as $10,000.[15]

Near the end of the summer in 1965, James Depue joined Kimbrell-Lawrence as an operations manager and to solicit cargo. He had a first-class resumé for employment in a company that seemed determined to expand. Depue had graduated from the U.S. Maritime Academy, operated a freezer boat in Alaska, worked on tugboats in Puget Sound, and in 1964, worked for Sea-Land Service in setting up its container-ship service between Seattle and Anchorage.[16] For whatever reasons, however, Depue stayed with Kimbrell-Lawrence Transportation for only about six months. His last position was as third mate on the *Western Pioneer*.[17]

Expansion at Kimbrell-Lawrence came in 1967 and was predicated on what Kimbrell recognized as the "tremendous current and potential growth of the king crab and other fisheries in Southwestern Alaska."[18] A concrete example of the ongoing growth was the construction in 1966, by Pan-Alaska Fisheries, of a $1 million crab-processing plant at Unalaska. The plant was capable of processing and freezing between 12,000 and 15,000 individual crabs per day. The plant was the first in the Aleutians, and perhaps Alaska, to produce frozen king crab sections ("clusters")—the legs, claw, and shoulder area from one side of a crab, all attached—rather than blocks of frozen crab meat. In reporting on the new plant, *Pacific Fisherman* observed that the fishing industry was turning Unalaska "from a quiet, rundown village into a money town."[19] By 1969, there were four crab-processing operations at Unalaska.[20] More would follow.

Frozen sections soon became the standard form in which king crab were sold. This change presented a problem

---

b   The dock at Bellingham Cold Storage was not unionized.

for cargo carriers because, on a weight basis, crab sections take up about twice as much space in a cargo hold as crab meat. Freight rates were typically based on poundage, so a hold full of crab sections would produce only about half the freight revenue as a hold full of blocks of crab meat. Kimbrell-Lawrence Transportation was at first reluctant to transport crab sections, but accommodated the new product by simply raising its rates on crab sections to a level that provided revenues about equal to those received from transporting frozen crab meat. Processors were able to absorb this increase in transportation cost.

The processors' switch from crab meat to crab sections effectively doubled the demand for cargo space. But there was more at play because the crab harvest was also growing. For transporters, it was a win-win situation: an increasing amount of crab was being caught, and it was being processed into a product that required a lot of cargo space. The Aleutian trade would expand in response.

While the Bering Sea crab industry boomed, a major shrimp fishery developed along the Pacific Ocean side of the southern Alaska Peninsula. Trawlers in 1968 began catching quantities of pink shrimp (*Pandalus borealis*), a small "cocktail" variety, and Peter Pan Seafoods began canning them at Squaw Harbor the following year. The shrimp were canned in half-pound cans that were packaged 48 cans to the case.

A portion of the company's production was regularly transported to Seattle aboard the *Western Pioneer*, though shipments, at least initially, tended to be less than 20 tons. Squaw Harbor was usually the vessel's last stop before heading south, and palletized cases of shrimp were carried beneath tarps on the back deck. Individual cases were hand-stowed in lockers beneath the shelter deck, as well as in containers that were sometimes carried on deck.[21]

At least one time, however, the *Western Pioneer*'s entire cargo was canned shrimp, and it made for many hours of hard work. Pallets of shrimp were lowered into each hold, and then, with gravity rollers as the only mechanical assistance, each case—it would have taken nearly 80,000 cases to make 2 million pounds—was individually hand-stowed until the vessel's holds were full to the deck beams. Unloading the cargo in Seattle took fully four days.[22]

The regional catch of pink shrimp peaked at nearly 50 million pounds during the 1977-78 season, but stocks soon began such a steep decline that the fishery was closed completely in 1980.[23]

The Aleutian Subsidy

Unalaska may have provided the bulk of the cargo that the *Western Pioneer* carried, but there were a considerable number of smaller outports that also relied on the vessel's services, particularly after 1964, when the federal government discontinued subsidized mailboat service that originated in Seward or Kodiak. Some communities, such as Ivanof Bay and Perryville, were off the *Western Pioneer*'s main route and usually had relatively small volumes of cargo. Providing service to them was often an economically marginal or even money-losing proposition. Carl Moses, a Dutch Harbor businessman of Aleut ancestry who had been elected in 1965 to represent District 12 in Alaska's House of Representatives, was acutely aware of the need of his constituents for reliable freight service, and in 1968 he was able to make considerable progress through the give-and-take of the legislative process.[c]

Alaska Governor Walter Hickel at the time was working to speed development on the state's North Slope, and Moses, in exchange for supporting the governor's proposal to bulldoze a one-shot road (Hickel Highway) to move oil-exploration equipment from Fairbanks to the North Slope, secured a line-item budget appropriation to directly subsidize the *Western Pioneer*'s service to outports in the Aleutian Islands area.[24] The Aleutian Subsidy, as it was called, was administered by the state's Department of Public Works, and was initially paid at a rate of $10 for each mile the *Western Pioneer* traveled from the main sea lane into an outport and back to the main lane.[25]

Kimbrell-Lawrence Transportation's business was growing, and to increase its cargo capacity, the company signed a contract with Alaska Steamship Co. to charter its onetime competition, the former Navy stores ship *Lucidor*.[26] (Angus Whyte, who worked for Kimbrell-Lawrence at

---

c District 12 at that time included the Alaska Peninsula, the Aleutian Islands, and the Pribilof Islands.

the time, characterized the arrangement as a "handshake partnership" between Ed Kimbrell and Alaska Steamship's D. E. Skinner.[27]) Alaska Steamship may have been amenable to the venture because it had lost the *Oduna* in November 1965, and it wanted to keep a presence in the Aleutian trade. (The 441-foot *Oduna*, which was carrying some $250,000 worth of frozen king crab, had grounded on a rock outcropping on the east side of Unimak Island in heavy seas during a snowstorm. She remains there to this day.)[28] No one had more experience in serving the growing Bering Sea king crab industry than Kimbrell and Lawrence.

The *Lucidor* (former *AF-45*) had been launched in 1945. She was 338 feet long, with a beam of 50 feet and a draft of 18 feet. A 1,700-horsepower Nordberg diesel main engine provided for a maximum speed of 12 knots. The vessel was renamed *Polar Pioneer* and, at Alaska Steamship's expense, underwent extensive renovations that were said to cost $750,000.[29] Design specifications were formulated by Ed Kimbrell in concert with W. C. Nickum and Sons, naval architects. When complete, the *Polar Pioneer* had been fitted with main engine controls on the bridge and a 6-foot-diameter bow thruster that was powered by a 600-horsepower diesel engine (the first such installation for use in Alaska waters). Additionally, concrete floors had been poured into the holds to enable the use of electric forklifts. She had 108,000 cubic feet of refrigerated cargo space below deck, and she was reported to be capable of carrying about 4 million pounds of frozen king crab plus about 20,000 cases of canned salmon.[30]

Befitting the names of the vessels it operated, Kimbrell-Lawrence Transportation began doing business as Pioneer Alaska Line. The firm also changed its funnel marking. The *Western Pioneer*'s funnel had been all red. Both vessels now had blue funnels inscribed with "PAL" in large white letters.[31] With two ships in its fleet, the company planned to offer departures from Seattle on the first and fifteenth day of each month.

The *Polar Pioneer* may have been operated by Kimbrell-Lawrence, but the service it offered was more in the tradition of Alaska Steamship than the versatile service that the *Western Pioneer* provided. The *Polar Pioneer* was expensive to operate and suitable mostly for carrying relatively large cargoes to a limited number of destinations.

With Paul Odsen at the helm, the *Polar Pioneer* departed on her maiden voyage on July 3, 1967.[32] For whatever reasons, Kimbrell and Lawrence's plans for monthly sailings of *Polar Pioneer* did not pan out. In January 1969, *Marine Digest* reported that the vessel operated only during the spring and summer.[33]

Not so with the *Western Pioneer*, which continued to make monthly departures year-round to the Aleutian Islands area. Everyone, particularly *Marine Digest*, seemed to look upon the *Western Pioneer* with affection.[d] She was the "little wood ship [that] defies Alaska's stormy seas" (*Alaska Industry*), the "plucky little trader," "one of the most rugged wooden vessels of her time," the "stout little ship . . . [that] can take almost any kind of weather in stride," and a "hard working . . . rugged little vessel" that had "weathered some strandings that would have sent most vessels to Davy Jones Locker" (*Marine Digest*). The *Western Pioneer* was also, of course, a "Gallant Ship" (U.S. government).[34] Even a mishap was used as an opportunity to praise the vessel. In November 1968, the *Western Pioneer* struck some rocks in the Shumagin Islands, damaging her hull and ripping out 75 feet of her starboard keel. Yet the vessel completed her voyage before returning to Seattle for $100,000 worth of repairs. Writer Don Page, of the *Seattle Post-Intelligencer*, was of the opinion that she survived because of her heavy wooden construction, and that this might not have been the case with a steel-hulled vessel.[35]

If being appointed by one's peers to head the Seattle Propeller Club's committee to judge the group's annual "Miss Maritime" competition was any kind of criterion, Ed Kimbrell was well respected in Seattle's maritime community, for that was exactly the honor bestowed upon him in 1968.[36] Associates in the industry later characterized Kimbrell as very personable but particularly ruthless when collecting overdue invoices.[37]

It seems that about this time, though it may have been a

---

d   Angus Whyte, who worked for Kimbrell-Lawrence Transportation for eight years, recalled that a writer from *Marine Digest* visited the company's office several times each month.

few years earlier, Captain Frank Buckler became the part-time master of the *Western Pioneer*. Buckler had come up through the ranks on Alaska Steamship vessels, had an unlimited tonnage master's license, and was a marine surveyor as well. Part of his reason for taking a position on the *Western Pioneer* seemed to be a desire for adventure.[38]

Alaska Industry in 1969 presented a sampling of northbound *Western Pioneer* cargo: "staples, fishing gear, homewares, contractors' supplies, airplane parts, poultry, livestock, pineapples and vast quantities of lumber. She may have a deckload of set up king crab pots, a load of piling up to 75 or 80 feet long, or hundreds of cylinders of propane and other compressed gasses."[39]

Linne Bardarson, who was superintendent of the New England Fish Co's crab-processing operation at Captains Bay (Unalaska), recalled that the *Western Pioneer*'s freight service was "the only game in town." He said that the vessel tried to keep its schedule, and that he communicated with it via single sideband radio.[40]

The year 1970 was one of change at Kimbrell-Lawrence Transportation. In February, the company ceased advertising monthly sailings of the *Polar Pioneer*.[41] The demise of the underutilized vessel was due, at least in part, to the inability of the operators to reach an agreement with the unions on the number of crewmembers that were required to man the ship.[42] Another likely factor was that Alaska Steamship was going out of business. By the fall of 1970, the once-proud line was reduced to operating only two vessels, and on January 30, 1971, the company ceased operations entirely.[43] D. E. Skinner, president of Alaska Steamship, blamed "economical factors" and a "dog-eat-dog competitive fight for the cream of the Alaska business."[e] [44] After spending some time laid up in Lake Washington, the *Polar Pioneer* was sold to a California firm.[45] One participant in the industry thought that the *Polar Pioneer* had been a good idea, but was about three years ahead of its time. The production of king crab sections was growing quickly when the *Polar Pioneer* was put into service,

but had not yet reached the point where the very substantial capacity it provided was necessary.[46]

Another factor behind the *Polar Pioneer*'s demise may have been rumors that Sea-Land Service might begin service to Unalaska. A student writing in the local paper thought that if this happened, freight rates would decrease and the *Western Pioneer* would be "almost or completely out of business."[47]

Closer to home, Kimbrell-Lawrence Transportation lost a lawsuit filed by one of its customers, Pan-Alaska Fisheries, over 11,000 pounds of frozen "fancy" king crab meat that was ruined or damaged in heavy weather encountered by the *Western Pioneer* en route to Puget Sound during February 1970. Water had found its way into the vessel's forward cargo hold. Kimbrell-Lawrence's attorney argued that the weather experienced by the *Western Pioneer*—sustained winds of 41 to 63 knots—was extraordinary and was to blame for the problem. The court found this argument unconvincing. During the trial, Alaska Steamship Captain Otto Karbbe, who had made at least 80 trips to Adak, testified for the plaintiff. Karbbe said that winds of the sort encountered by the *Western Pioneer* were not extraordinary, and noted that the vessel itself had suffered no damage. Pan-Alaska claimed only $15,477.10 in damages, but the cost of the lawsuit in terms of customer relations must have been significant.[48]

Finally, 1970 was the year that Richard Lawrence bought Ed Kimbrell's interest in Kimbrell-Lawrence Transportation.[49] Angus Whyte, the company's freight manager, was present at the summer meeting in which Kimbrell—for reasons unknown to Whyte—abruptly announced to Lawrence that one partner should buy the other out. Whyte thought that Kimbrell intended to purchase Lawrence's share, but in the end, Lawrence paid Kimbrell $125,000 to become the sole owner of Kimbrell-Lawrence Transportation. After the purchase, Lawrence confided to a colleague that he intended to operate the business for about a year, then sell it and retire.[50]

Not long after he purchased the company, Richard Lawrence moved its Seattle operation from Pier 66 to Pier 42, which had formerly been occupied by Alaska Steamship. Pier 42, like Pier 66, was a "union dock," where it was required that union longshoremen (ILWU) load and unload vessels.[51]

---

e   Alaska Steamship had lost the bulk of its business to Sea-Land Service, which in 1964 began operating weekly container ships between Seattle and Anchorage.

The *Western Pioneer*
in drydock.

CHAPTER 5

Western Pioneer, the Business

THE *WESTERN PIONEER* WAS ONE OF THE LAST WOOD-HULLED FREIGHTERS ON THE WEST COAST, and the last in the Alaska trade. It had served well, and continued to do so, with full loads of cargo being the norm. But Richard Lawrence, after less than two years as sole owner of the business (a little longer than he had intended), wanted out. He offered to sell it, including the *Western Pioneer*, to Captain Paul Odsen and Angus Whyte for $250,000, but he received an offer of $300,000 from another interest. Odsen and Whyte matched the offer, but this was bettered by an offer of $350,000 from an old friend, Amigo Soriano. Lawrence and Soriano had been shipmates many years before on the Alaska Steamship vessel *Aleutian*. The business was sold in the late summer of 1972 to Swiftsure, a Seattle corporation owned by Amigo Soriano and four of his five brothers—Dewey, Max, Milton, and Rupert. The corporation had a host of real estate investments in Seattle. The brothers' venture into the maritime transportation industry was led by Amigo, who was assisted by his brother Max.

Amigo was supremely qualified to run the operation. He had a wealth of experience in maritime matters, some of which would have caused a less stout-hearted individual to swear off going to sea.

The eldest of 10 children, Amigo was born in Ketchikan in 1915. His father owned a halibut schooner, and Amigo began going to sea with him when he was only five years old. When Amigo was a teenager during Prohibition, he and his father ran rum—1,000 cases at a time—from Mexico to Northern California. In 1934, he shipped out as a seaman. In May 1942, he was second mate on the U.S.-registered freighter *Ogontz*,

A former captain for Alaska Steamship Co. and a Puget Sound ship pilot, Amigo Soriano was a good fit at the helm of Western Pioneer.

which was carrying nitrates from Chile to Mobile, Alabama. The vessel was torpedoed and sunk by a German submarine in the Gulf of Mexico. Those who could reach lifeboats got in and rowed away. Amigo and a shipmate were left behind. To their great surprise, the submarine surfaced nearby, took them aboard, and delivered them to a lifeboat. Before the submarine departed, a German pointed in the direction of Mexico and wished them luck.[1]

Amigo became one of the youngest Alaska Steamship Co. masters ever.[2] Toward the end of the war, he was master of the Liberty ship *William T. Sherman*. With him were three of his brothers—Rupert, Dewey, and Milton—who were, respectively, chief mate, second mate, and third mate.[3]

In February 1946, Amigo was aboard the *Yukon*, an Alaska Steamship vessel transporting mostly military personnel from Alaska to Seattle. In a heavy gale accompanied by a blinding snowstorm, the *Yukon* ran aground on jagged rocks at Cape Fairfield, about 40 miles southeast of Seward. Eleven individuals perished, and the vessel was a total loss. Amigo was the vessel's pilot, but the captain, who had been awake for 30 hours, was at the helm when the vessel grounded.

From 1948 until 1952, Amigo worked in Seattle at Rothschild International Stevedoring, where he was in charge of loading and discharging cargo. In 1952, he became a Puget Sound pilot. His job was to board ships entering Puget Sound and use his skills and local knowledge to navigate them to their destination. He is remembered by others in the industry as one of the very best.[4] Amigo's brother Dewey also became a Puget Sound pilot.

Max Soriano had some experience at sea, including in Alaska, but was a lawyer by profession.

The Sorianos purchased the business simply because it looked to offer a good opportunity for profit. Their purchase was also a vote of confidence in the *Western Pioneer*.

The first step the Sorianos took was to change the business's name to Western Pioneer. They also moved the business from Pier 42 to Pier 91, where there were better warehouse facilities. Importantly, unlike Pier 42, Pier 91 was a nonunion dock, where operations could be conducted more economically. In 1973, the operation was moved to a leased four-acre site at what was called the Cedar Mill Dock, on the north shore of the Lake Washington Ship Canal just

The *Bowfin* high and dry in Bristol Bay, circa 1980s. Navigation errors were not uncommon. Fortunately, no damage was done, and the next high tide floated the vessel.

west of the Ballard Bridge. This location too was beyond the jurisdiction of the longshoremen's union (ILWU).[5]

Western Pioneer was a hands-on family operation in which everyone did whatever needed to be done. When the *Western Pioneer* was being loaded or unloaded at the company dock, Amigo might be running the cargo gear while his brother Max worked in the cargo hold. At times, the other Soriano brothers—Dewey, Rupert, and Milton—might show up to work in the hold, drive a forklift, or run the gear "for the fun of it." Millie, Amigo's wife, would prepare hearty sandwiches and snacks for lunch and coffee breaks for the ever-hungry longshore crews. Larry and Jim, Max's sons, began working on the dock and then going to sea on the company's boats when they were teenagers, and his daughter,

Liz, worked in the office answering the telephone and helping with billing and customer service. Four of Amigo's children—Steve, Sally, Marilyn, and Don—worked in different capacities for the family enterprise: going to sea, working in the office or warehouse, meeting with customers, and basically doing whatever they could to help build the family business.[6]

Though they were out of the business, Ed Kimbrell and Richard Lawrence would occasionally visit Western Pioneer's terminal to offer advice to Amigo Soriano. A former Western Pioneer employee recalled that either Kimbrell or Lawrence—he wasn't sure which one—retained his fondness for and pride in the *Western Pioneer* to the extent that during the summer he voluntarily painted the vessel's rails.

As required by law, the *Western Pioneer* had a U.S. Coast Guard Certificate of Inspection. It was operated by a crew of 14 to 16, all of whom were licensed by the Coast Guard and represented by various seafaring unions. The large crew was required because the *Western Pioneer* maintained a "three-watch" operation in which officers and men worked four hours on and eight hours off on a continuous basis.

It seems that Captain Paul Odsen, who had been master of the *Western Pioneer* under Kimbrell and Lawrence, made some trips early on for the Sorianos. Though qualified, Amigo Soriano did not operate the vessel, but would fly to Alaska if a problem arose.

The *Western Pioneer*'s four Cooper-Bessemer main engines each had six cylinders, so there was a total of 24 cylinders. A chief engineer on the boat had a novel engine-rebuilding schedule: after each trip, he rebuilt one cylinder. In that manner, assuming one trip per month, all 24 cylinders were rebuilt over two years. Then it was time to start over.[7]

In 1973, Western Pioneer added a second vessel, the *Dolphin*, to its roster.[a] With a length of only 135 feet and a hold capacity of only 13,000 cubic feet, the *Dolphin* was on the small side for the Aleutian trade. A fellow named Swede Parker had previously used her as a tramper between Puget Sound and ports in Alaska.[8] More recently, Vita Foods, from which she was purchased, had used her to ferry frozen king crab from floating processors at Adak to Dutch Harbor.[9]

a   This vessel was referred to as the *"Little" Dolphin* to distinguish it from a larger vessel later acquired by Western Pioneer and renamed *Dolphin*.

Bowfin, a typical Western Pioneer "YO" freighter, circa 1980s. The *Bowfin* was fitted with traditional yard-and-stay cargo gear. On some of the vessels in Western Pioneer's YO fleet, however, the yard-and-stay gear was replaced with articulated hydraulic cranes (see page 56).

Max Soriano, an attorney and one of the principal owners of Western Pioneer, was no stranger to physical labor. Like his brothers, Max did whatever was necessary to keep the company's freight moving. In this image frozen salmon is being discharged from the *Pribilof* circa 1980s.

The *Dolphin* once returned from a voyage with a number of pilothouse windows broken out. During some especially severe weather, a huge wave had smashed into the house with such force that it took out the front windows. The torrent of water that washed through the house was so strong that it swept two crewmembers down the stairwell and broke out two rear windows. A young dockworker at Western Pioneer had aspirations to go to sea, but they evaporated when he saw the damage the *Dolphin* had endured.[10]

Being on the small side in the Alaska trade had one advantage, and it was a big one. In 1968, Congress had passed legislation that exempted cannery and fishing tender vessels of not more than 500 gross tons in the salmon and crab fisheries of Oregon, Washington, and Alaska from Coast Guard inspection requirements. As broadly defined by Congress, cannery and fishing tender vessels included those engaged exclusively in the "carriage of cargo to or from vessels in the fishery or a facility used or to be used in the processing or assembling of fishery products."[11]

Vessels subject to inspection by the Coast Guard, on the other hand, must comply with a broad array of structural and equipment requirements. Among them are detailed specifications regarding the vessel's construction and arrangement, its equipment, wiring, stability, fire protection, lifesaving gear, and vessel manning and operation. Many of the requirements are costly, and together can easily make the difference between a profitable vessel operation and an uneconomic one. This is particularly true if an existing, noncomplying vessel must be retrofitted in order to comply.[12] A vessel passing inspection is issued a Coast Guard Certificate of Inspection (COI), which is valid for five years but requires annual inspections.

This exemption granted by Congress was critical to the development and survival of what was sometimes referred to as Alaska's "mosquito fleet," but it made no provision for the transport of cargo not related to the fishing industry. The accepted—though technically fraudulent—method of skirting the law was to consign all cargo to fishing industry vessels, no matter to whom or for what end it was actually destined.

The *Dolphin* was eventually sold off, and in 1975 Western Pioneer acquired a former World War II U.S. Navy yard oiler (YO) that was designed to refuel warships at dockside. The 156-foot vessel was converted to haul general and refrigerated cargo and renamed *Marlin*.

YO conversions became the basis of Western Pioneer's fleet. The vessels—which had been constructed for the Navy in two sizes, 156 feet and 174 feet—were less than 500 gross registered tons, relatively inexpensive, and very well built. Converting them to carry freight was fairly straightforward. In all, Western Pioneer converted six YOs into freighters for the Aleutian trade.[b] All except the *Marlin* were 174-footers, and each consumed about 20 to 22 thousand gallons of diesel fuel per Alaska voyage.[13]

---

b *Bowfin, Capelin, "Big" Dolphin, Marlin, Sculpin,* and *Tarpon.*

Aleutian cargo operations during the 1980s were typically carried out while at anchor. Here, the Western Pioneer vessel *Tarpon*, fitted with articulated hydraulic cranes to move cargo, is tied alongside a "Knot ship" that is most likely anchored in Akutan Harbor. Knot ships were the smaller cousins of the famous World War II-era Liberty ships. Many Knot ships were converted to fish processors.

CHAPTER 6

New Entrants into the Trade: Alaska Marine Charters and Aleut Alaska Shipping

ALASKA MARINE CHARTERS

Unlike Kimbrell and Lawrence, the Sorianos did not have the Aleutian Islands area niche market to themselves for very long. Angus Whyte, who with Paul Odsen had been outbid by the Sorianos in their attempt to purchase the *Western Pioneer*, had a solid knowledge of the business and the customer base. Whyte saw in the dramatic growth of the king crab fishery a great need for additional transport capacity. He would have preferred to go into business himself, but could not afford to do so. He found partners in Lee Huard and Robert and Herman Schoenbacker, and together in February 1975 they formed Alaska Marine Charters, Inc.

The company purchased the 185-foot king crab boat *Apollo*, which had originally been built as a Navy supply vessel, and converted it into a freighter while it was tied to a dock in Ballard. In the process, the holds were insulated and refrigerated, two 40-foot refrigerated containers were mounted just aft of the pilothouse, and more generating capacity was added. The vessel was renamed *Snowbird*. In all, it had a little less than 30,000 cubic feet of refrigerated space and a capacity of about 700 tons, and had cost about $600,000.

The *Snowbird*'s first trip was in the summer of 1975. It was a financial disaster. Potential customers had little faith in the fledgling operation, and the vessel left Seattle only half loaded. It returned empty. The dismayed owners scheduled a second trip, which fortunately was an improvement over the first. Gradually, Alaska Marine Charters built up a clientele and began operating the *Snowbird* on a year-round monthly schedule from Seattle to ports extending from Kodiak to the Dutch Harbor area. Like Western Pioneer's vessels, the *Snowbird* transported individual lots of cargo that would have been prohibitively expensive on a carrier charging for van-load lots.[1] It operated with a crew of five and consumed about 18,000 to 19,000 gallons of diesel fuel per voyage.[2]

Alaska Marine Charters originally leased a small dock and warehouse on the north shore of the Lake Washington Ship Canal just west of the Ballard Bridge. The City of Seattle had wanted to lease the company space at Pier 66, but the pier was unionized, and Alaska Marine Charters wanted to avoid the high cost of having its vessel loaded by union labor. The dock the company was using, however, was just too small to work, so operations were moved to Pier 1, on Harbor Island, which is in the mouth of the Duwamish River, south of downtown Seattle. This facility was unionized, but longshoremen there didn't object to Alaska Marine Charters loading its "puddlejumper" with nonunion labor.[3]

SEA STORY NO. 1

In the fall of 1976, the *Snowbird* was en route from Dutch Harbor to Seattle with a full load of frozen crab. A major storm was raging, and near the Queen Charlotte Islands she was hit by a rogue wave that took out her pilothouse windows and left two feet of water in the wheelhouse. Fearful of being electrocuted, Doug Surwold, the captain, climbed atop the pilothouse console to radio a mayday. The weather was so horrific, however, that the Coast Guard refused to come to his assistance. Fortunately, the container ship *Great Land* was not far away. The 791-foot vessel slowed to approach and assist, but was herself hit by an especially large wave. Her captain determined that there was nothing he could do to help the imperiled *Snowbird*. Despite the damage, the *Snowbird*'s main systems continued to function, and she managed to make it into the Inside Passage on her own. She then proceeded to Juneau, where the crew fashioned makeshift windows out of plywood and Plexiglas. Several days later the *Snowbird* arrived safely in Seattle. But the ordeal was not yet over. Before she was unloaded, two armed federal marshals arrived at Alaska Marine Charters' dock and placed a lien for $525,000 on the *Snowbird*. It was on behalf of the owners of the *Great Land*, Totem Ocean Trailer Express (TOTE). The big wave that struck the *Great Land* during her aborted effort to help the *Snowbird* had caused a lot of damage. TOTE claimed that the *Snowbird* was at fault. The *Kodiak Daily Mirror* wrote a scathing account of the ordeal, after which the lien was apparently dropped.[4]

ALEUT ALASKA SHIPPING CO.

In 1975, another business entered the trade. The Aleut Corporation, the for-profit Aleutian Islands/Pribilof Islands/lower Alaska Peninsula regional Native corporation established by the Alaska Native Claims Settlement Act (1971), purchased the vessel *Pribilof* from the U.S. Fish and Wildlife Service. At great cost to the government, the 205-foot *Pribilof* had been making some four annual trips between Seattle and the Pribilof Islands. It was cheaper for the government to sell the vessel to a private enterprise and then contract for the shipping. The terms of the sale were exceedingly favorable: $265,000 for the vessel, no down payment, no interest, and 10 years to pay.[5]

As part of the sale arrangement, the Aleut Corp. signed a 10-year contract with the government to make four annual trips between Seattle and the Pribilof Islands. A subsidiary firm, the Aleut Alaska Shipping Co., was formed to service the Pribilof Islands contract and to operate a common-carrier freight service to other Bering Sea area locations.

The *Pribilof* was not cheap to operate. Its Coast Guard Certificate of Inspection required a crew of 14, and all were union members. The vessel also used a lot of fuel.[6] Despite this, the *Pribilof*'s 1975 sailings, according to a State of Alaska

transportation report, had "proven economically successful."[7] At least on its first two voyages, the vessel was loaded to capacity both northbound and southbound.[8]

The Aleut Corp. lacked a dock and warehouse space in Seattle, and initially leased the *Pribilof* to Western Pioneer on a trip-by-trip basis. Amigo Soriano's brother Dewey operated the vessel for a couple of trips. The corporation also explored the possibility of entering into a joint venture with Western Pioneer in a firm that was to be called the Aleutian Transportation Co., but the Native corporation had some misgivings and decided against doing so.[9]

In 1976, however, the Aleut Corp. entered into a joint venture with Alaska Marine Charters, at which time Alaska Marine Charters changed its name to Alaska Marine Shipping (AMS).[10] The Aleut Corp. that year also acquired a second vessel, a former Navy yard oiler (YO) for which it paid $60,000.[11] About the same time, the *Pribilof* was renamed *Aleut Provider*, though it was later changed back to *Pribilof*.[12] The YO was converted into a 40,000-cubic-foot-capacity cargo ship at the Duwamish Shipyard, renamed *Aleut Packer*, and placed in service in March 1977.[13] Both the *Aleut Packer* and the *Pribilof* were regularly leased to and operated by AMS.

Though the effort was uncomfortable to say the least, AMS eventually ended union representation on the *Pribilof*.[14] In 1977, the expanding AMS moved its operations to a nonunionized facility known simply as "Jacobson's dock." This facility was located on the north shore of the Lake Washington Ship Canal just east of the Ballard Bridge, and it included a 450-foot dock and 18,000 square feet of warehouse space. Part of the reason for the move was that longshoremen at Pier 1 had insisted that the *Aleut Packer*, a more substantial vessel than the *Snowbird*, be loaded with union labor. A single loading once cost $14,000.[15]

In addition to servicing the Pribilof Islands, the *Snowbird*, *Pribilof*, and *Aleut Packer* mostly transported frozen crab. In what was a far cry from the company's initial foray into the transportation business, it now sometimes had to turn down cargo for lack of space. AMS's primary customer was Universal Seafoods (now UniSea), which began operating the crab-processing vessel *UniSea* at Dutch Harbor in 1975 and is today one of the largest seafood-processing

Snowbird, owned by Alaska Marine Charters, at Jacobson Terminal, Lake Washington Ship Canal, in the late 1970s.

companies in Alaska.[16] AMS usually reserved 14,000 cubic feet of southbound refrigerated cargo space on each *Snowbird* voyage for Universal Seafoods' product. Under an agreement with AMS, Universal Seafoods workers unloaded and loaded the *Snowbird*. This was greatly appreciated by the vessel's crew, which lobbied to increase Universal's allocation of space.[17] AMS also seasonally transported canned salmon.[18]

Prior to entering into the joint venture with the Aleut Corp., AMS did not maintain contact with the *Snowbird* while it was at sea. Soon after entering into the joint venture, however, the company installed a single sideband radio in its office and—atmospheric conditions permitting—maintained a daily 9:30 a.m. schedule with its three vessels.[19]

Industry Briefs, 1970-1979

TANNER CRAB

The crab industry in Alaska was growing robustly in the early 1970s. In addition to king crab, there were Tanner crab, a smaller and less valuable genus that fishermen had begun to target in the 1960s. Two species of Tanner crab are harvested by U.S. fishermen in the North Pacific: bairdi (*Chionoecetes bairdi*), which average about 2.5 pounds and are a favorite on the Japanese market, and opilio or "snow" crab (*Chionoecetes opilio*), which average about 1.5 pounds and are commonly the feature of all-you-can-eat crab buffets in the United States. In the Bering Sea, fishermen were initially mostly interested in bairdi, but began enthusiastically fishing "opies" in 1979, when the bairdi catch began to dwindle. That year, a growing Bering Sea fleet of some 160 U.S. vessels caught about 40 million pounds of bairdi and 20 million pounds of opilio.[20]

SEA-LAND SERVICE

During the mid 1970s, Unalaska/Dutch Harbor was a busy place. In 1975, there were 14 seafood-processing companies in operation, a situation described the following January as a "stabilized boom."[21] There was a lot of cargo moving in and out of what was rapidly becoming one of Alaska's major fishing ports. And there was suddenly an increase in competition to carry that cargo. To fill the void left by the demise of Alaska Steamship, Sea-Land Service in 1972 began carrying cargo between Seattle and the Navy base at Adak, and the company seems to have provided some service to Unalaska/Dutch Harbor on an as-needed basis with the *Summit*, which was capable of transporting both containers and break-bulk freight.[22] As well, some service to the community was being provided by tug and barge operations such as Red Stack and Puget Sound Tug & Barge.[23]

Sea-Land made a real commitment to servicing Unalaska/Dutch Harbor late in 1975, when it scheduled twice-monthly sailings to that port and others in the Aleutian Islands area by the ship *Aleutian Developer*. The vessel could carry 90 containers as well as break-bulk cargo. She would transship cargo from the Aleutian Islands area to Kodiak, which was a stop on Sea-Land's weekly run between Anchorage and Seattle.[24]

THE FATE OF THE ALEUTIAN SUBSIDY AND THE *WESTERN PIONEER*

The Aleutian Subsidy was a victim of the increased number of carriers to the Aleutian Islands area. By 1975, the subsidy had increased from its original $10 per mile to $19 per mile, and the following year it was again increased to $22 per mile.[25] Alaska's legislature appropriated $35,000 for the subsidy for fiscal year 1976.[26]

As far as the vessel *Western Pioneer* was concerned, however, the subsidy became a moot point, for in September or October of 1975, she caught fire while tied to the dock at Ballard. The fire was below deck, and sections of a number of deck beams were cut away to access it. The damage to the *Western Pioneer*'s structural integrity from the cutting was deemed so severe that she was written off as a total loss.

By this time, however, it was apparent to some that the subsidy was no longer necessary. Western Pioneer was operating its namesake vessel plus the *Dolphin* and *Marlin*. In addition, the company occasionally chartered the *Pribilof* from the Aleut Corp. As well, Western Pioneer's direct competition, Alaska Marine Charters, was operating the *Snowbird* along roughly the same route, and additional

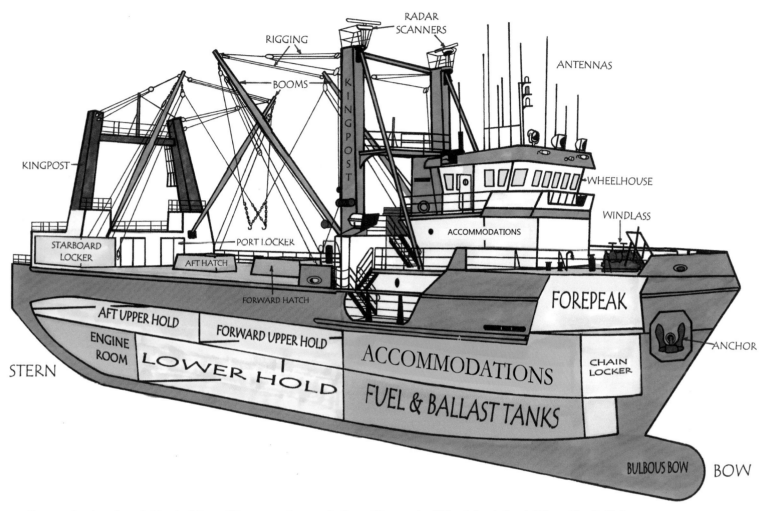

Cutaway drawing of nearly identical Coastal Transportation vessels *Coastal Progress* (ex-*Yellowfin*) **and** *Coastal Nomad* (ex-*Redfin*).

vessels were scheduled to come on line. A State of Alaska contracted study in 1976 recommended that the need for the Aleutian Subsidy be re-examined, based on the "well-paying backhaul of processed fish and shellfish now available, the increasing amount of inbound freight, and the number of carriers actually vying for the trade."[27] Alaska's legislature seems to have terminated the Aleutian Subsidy soon afterward.

The loss of the *Western Pioneer* was in a way convenient, for the venerable and supremely capable vessel had become something of a liability. It was prohibitively expensive

to operate in comparison to the company's fleet of YO conversions, which being under 500 gross tons, did not require a Coast Guard Certificate of Inspection. The loss of the *Western Pioneer* also ended union representation at Western Pioneer, except for the occasions when the company operated the *Pribilof*.

The vessel that had made nearly 200 voyages between Seattle and the Aleutian Islands area was later sold by the insurance company for about $11,000.[28] It was eventually repaired and used for a number of years to transport cargo between Puget Sound and Alaska for Whitney-Fidalgo Seafoods.[29]

By the 1970s, the optimal size and configuration of Aleutian freighters had emerged. The vessels needed to be less than 260 feet long to fit the short docks typical in the region, and to have two to four refrigerated cargo holds to segregate cargo for different ports. Rapid loading and discharging of cargo was accomplished with two sets of yard-and-stay cargo gear, or, in the case of some Western Pioneer freighters, articulated hydraulic cranes. Shown is an illustration of the *Coastal Trader* (ex-*Sunmar Sky*) from Coastal Transportation's training manual *Seamanship for Beginners*.

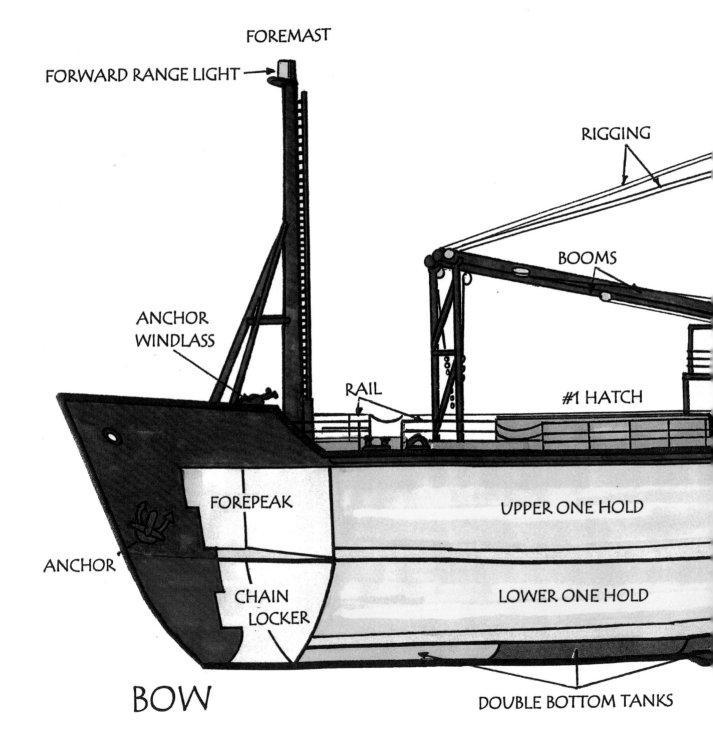

FOREMAST

FORWARD RANGE LIGHT

RIGGING

BOOMS

ANCHOR WINDLASS

RAIL

#1 HATCH

FOREPEAK

UPPER ONE HOLD

ANCHOR

CHAIN LOCKER

LOWER ONE HOLD

DOUBLE BOTTOM TANKS

BOW

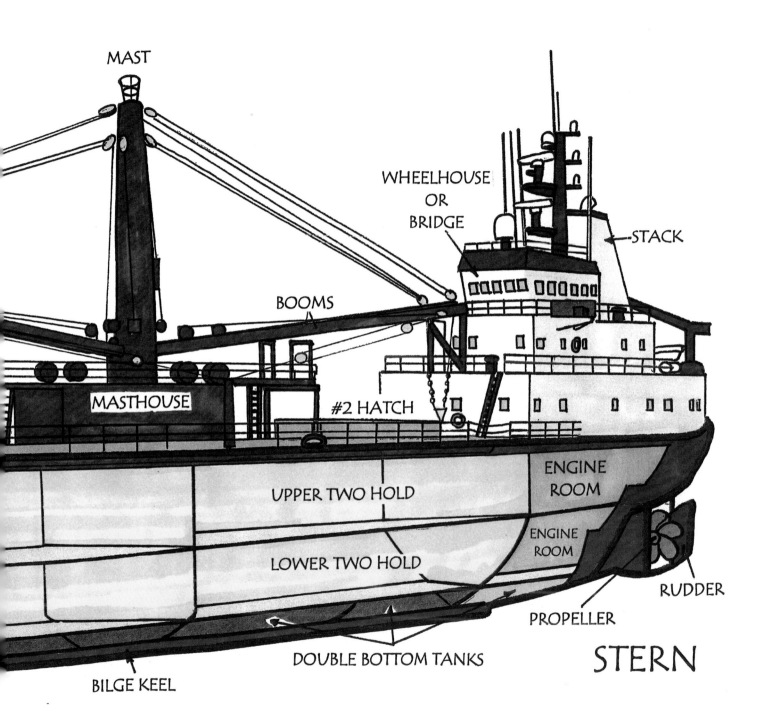

MAST

WHEELHOUSE
OR
BRIDGE

STACK

BOOMS

MASTHOUSE

#2 HATCH

ENGINE
ROOM

UPPER TWO HOLD

ENGINE
ROOM

LOWER TWO HOLD

RUDDER

PROPELLER

DOUBLE BOTTOM TANKS

STERN

BILGE KEEL

Part of an eight-person crew of the Western Pioneer vessel *Sculpin* during the 1980s. Willy Cork (second from left), Jed Arnold (second from right), and David Sanders (right) later became marine pilots, the specialists who navigate large deep-sea vessels into and out of port.

Captains, Crewmen, Recreation, and Alcohol

OBTAINING QUALIFIED OFFICERS FOR THE ALEUTIAN TRADE

There was a problem manning this growing "mosquito fleet." Coast Guard regulations required that the captain, first mate, and engineer be licensed, but there were few licensed captains who were willing to take a small ship to the remote and perilous waters of the Aleutian Islands area, particularly during the winter. Simply put, they could usually find better work. Those who were available were sometimes nearing the end of their careers or had other issues, like alcoholism. Yet, if Western Pioneer's boats were to operate and the fleet to grow, Amigo Soriano needed captains. The manner in which he obtained them produced results that persist to this day.

Soriano resided in West Seattle and began recruiting young men from the neighborhood to work on the boats. He particularly cultivated those who he thought had the intelligence and mettle to be captains, and he quickly gave these individuals as much responsibility as they were willing and able to handle—"as much rope as they could drag," in the words of a former company captain.[1] Young men hired as seamen became deck officers and then captains as soon as they qualified. Major responsibility sometimes came quickly. One former captain recalled that as a young first mate, he once locked his drunken captain in a room and took control of the vessel. It was, he said, just a part of the job that he had to be prepared to do; the vessel couldn't come to a halt simply because its captain was incapacitated.

Soriano wasn't paternalistic or mentoring toward his men on the boats. His was more of a man-to-man/get-the-job-done relationship, but he did make them aware of the opportunity that working for him presented. They were accumulating valuable experience and sea time at a very young age. Once they became captains, there would be opportunities to move on to more prestigious positions. A considerable

number heeded his advice and example. Nearly a dozen of the young neighborhood men he brought into the industry chose to follow in his footsteps to become Puget Sound pilots. In a world in which Puget Sound pilots had been, almost to a man, older veterans of many years at sea, some former Western Pioneer captains obtained their Puget Sound pilot licenses while in their early 30s. Amigo Soriano's greatest legacy may be that he provided the avenue that led so many young men into positions of great responsibility.

Angus Whyte, at Alaska Marine Shipping (AMS), likewise had some difficulty finding qualified captains and mates for the *Snowbird* and *Aleut Packer*, but he resolved the issue differently than Soriano. (The *Pribilof* was a Coast Guard–inspected vessel, and thus subject to different manning requirements.) To operate the *Snowbird* and *Aleut Packer*, Whyte chose to cultivate Alaska commercial fishermen who had the proper licenses.

The captains who worked for AMS were originally paid $150 for each day at sea. While this wage was eventually raised to $175 per day, the captains actually wanted $200. Whyte began to notice that their voyages were taking more

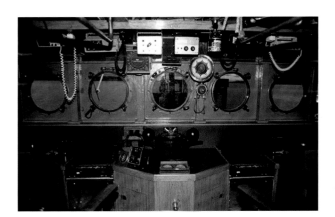

The cramped interior of a converted "YO" freighter's wheelhouse.

VERY HARD WORK

The operation of a small break-bulk freighter is labor intensive in the extreme, but a typical trip doesn't start that way. Absent emergencies, the five-day voyage from Seattle to the first port serviced, perhaps Chignik, is likened to a vacation. There is a routine. The captain and first mate navigate while the deck and engine-room crews do routine maintenance, so far as it can be done at sea. The cook prepares three meals a day. There is time to relax, perhaps by reading or watching a movie.

The routine ends on approach to the first port, when the crew begins readying the deck gear and the cargo to be discharged. If the cargo was properly marked and loaded in Seattle, it shouldn't be difficult to retrieve and unload. Southbound or interport cargo is then taken aboard and secured. Then it's off to a succession of ports—perhaps a dozen of them—where the exercise is repeated. Such is the routine until the vessel is finally under way for Seattle.

Loading large cargoes of frozen product can be a brutal process that leaves even the strongest individuals completely exhausted. It was particularly hard prior to the early 1990s, when frozen crab sections were often packed 100 net pounds to the box. A 1.5-million-pound cargo would amount to about 14,000 individual boxes. To maximize the utilization of the vessel's cargo space, the boxes were individually hand stacked in the holds. George Collazo, Coastal Transportation's port captain, explained that a crewmember working cargo was expected to be almost superhuman. He had to be able to lift a 100-pound box of crab to shoulder height and to continually stack identical boxes for a full 24 hours, the only breaks being an hour to eat every six hours, and 15 minutes to use the bathroom every three hours. And that was just the beginning: after just four hours of sleep, he would be expected to repeat the 24-hour work routine. But even then, the job was not yet finished: after six hours of sleep, there would be 16 more hours of stacking crab.[3] Doctors have told Collazo that a person simply couldn't work that hard and long. Collazo knew they could. He had done so himself.

Today, 100-pound boxes are rarely used, but every so often crews find themselves stacking 50-pound boxes on the same schedule.

A fully laden *Yellowfin* (later *Coastal Progress*) under way in Unimak Pass. Mount Shishaldin is in the background.

time than he thought necessary. He knew that the *Western Pioneer* had been making the voyage in 26 to 28 days. AMS's *Snowbird*, with considerably less cargo to discharge and load, was taking 24 days. Whyte believed the trips were being prolonged because the captains and crews wanted more time on the payroll. This was costly; fewer trips could be made in a given period of time, and in addition to the increase in labor costs, there were also increased costs for items such as fuel and food. To end this practice, Whyte made an offer to the captains: he would pay them an annual salary of $73,000, equal to $200 per day for each and every day of the year, at sea or not, provided they would agree to make up to 12 voyages annually. (A deckhand on a king crab boat at that time could earn $40,000 a year.) They accepted, and the end result was a win-win situation. The vessels usually completed voyages in 19 or 20 days, the number of annual voyages made by the *Snowbird* increased from 8 to 12, and the captains got to spend about the same amount of time at home but with more money in their pockets.[2]

In July 1983, Jack Miller (red shirt) and some *Tarpon* crewmembers spent several hours exploring Icy Bay (on the Gulf of Alaska, just west of Yakutat) in Miller's skiff while the *Tarpon* proceeded toward a rendezvous with a floating crab processor that was anchored in Icy Bay.

CLOCKWISE FROM TOP LEFT:

Pat Carlo, captain of the Western Pioneer vessel *Dolphin*, circa 1980s.

Dolphin deckhand Taylor Campbell (later Western Pioneer Company and Coastal Transportation, Inc., captain) in the 1980s. Once the vessel's cargo is secured, a deckhand's work on an Aleutian freighter is the same as that of any other ship—maintenance and painting.

Chief Engineer Ed Olson at work in the *Dolphin*'s engine room in the 1980s. Today, an Aleutian freighter crew typically includes a licensed chief engineer and an unlicensed assistant engineer.

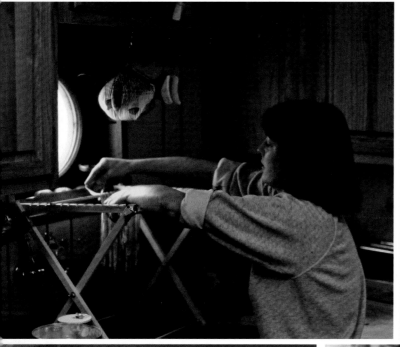

CLOCKWISE FROM LEFT:

In the *Dolphin*'s galley, cook Pam Aus prepares fish for smoking. At sea, meals are both nourishment and entertainment, and good cooks are treasured. Aus recorded life aboard Aleutian freighters during the 1980s with a camera, and she provided many of the images in this book.

Willy Cork in the cab of one of the *Sculpin*'s articulated hydraulic cranes in the 1980s. The installation of these cranes on some of Western Pioneer's freighters proved to be something of a mistake. Two people were required to operate them—a crane driver in the cab and a signaler. The traditional arrangement of booms ("yard-and-stay" cargo gear) requires only a gear operator, and this method provides better load control, an important factor when taking cargo at anchor.

Symbol of an era: an exhausted man with a fish box. After a pallet of frozen cargo was lowered into the hold, a battery-powered pallet jack was used to maneuver it to where the real work—"handstacking"—began. With box weights often over a hundred pounds, handstacking boxes to the hold's overhead was a brutal endurance marathon. Beginning in the mid 1990s, handstacking was mostly replaced by the use of battery-powered forklifts that were lowered into the hold to stack entire pallets.

While en route from Dutch Harbor to Seattle on a beautiful summer day in 1983, the Western Pioneer vessel *Tarpon* made a side trip into Icy Bay to load frozen Dungeness crab from a floating processor. Mount St. Elias, Alaska's second-highest peak, is in the background.

RECREATION

As long as the job got done, Soriano was pretty tolerant of his crews' "extracurricular" activities. With young crews working independently, there were bound to be some liberties taken. Vessels would sometimes divert to a favored location to spend some time fishing, or when they crossed paths with another Western Pioneer vessel, to anchor and go ashore for a baseball game on the beach. On one summer voyage of the *Tarpon* in the early 1980s, Jack Miller, a West Seattle friend of some of the crewmembers as well as Amigo Soriano, went along for the ride. He brought his 20-foot skiff. Weather permitting, the standard daily procedure while traveling was to put Jack's skiff over the side in the morning so Jack and several crewmembers could spend the day exploring the beaches while the *Tarpon* continued along its course. Communication was maintained between the skiff and the *Tarpon* by VHF radio. In the evening the skiff and its crew would be hoisted on deck to get a good meal and a good night's sleep in preparation for the next day's adventures.

ALCOHOLIC BEVERAGES

Though it didn't seem to be a problem among the younger crewmen, there was always alcohol on the boats. Under federal law, a liberal amount of "sea stores" liquor, wine, and beer (as well as cigarettes)—to be consumed in Canada or beyond the three-mile limit—could be purchased tax free in Seattle. A federal official sealed the purchases upon delivery to the vessel, but there seemed to be little enforcement of the consumption provision: the seals were often broken as soon as the vessel cleared the Ballard locks, and folks pretty much consumed the beverages as they pleased and where they pleased. At times Western Pioneer vessels were amply supplied with sea stores at company expense, and the captains were instructed to pass out bottles to customers along the route as gifts of appreciation for their business. At Coastal Transportation (CTI), which joined Western Pioneer in serving the Aleutian Islands area in 1984 (see Chapter 9), individual crewmen sometimes brought a supply of alcohol to sell at ports along the way. This was reminiscent of the entrepreneurial spirit of the first mate on the *Starr* a half century earlier.

Alcohol consumption on vessels has long been a recognized problem. The issue really came to a head in the United States, however, in 1989, after the oil tanker *Exxon Valdez* fetched up on Bligh Reef in Prince William Sound. Exxon, a major U.S. corporation with vast resources, had employed Captain Joseph Hazelwood, a lapsed alcoholic, as master of the tanker. On March 23, 1989, Hazelwood was seen drinking in a local establishment not long before the 987-foot vessel, laden with 53 million gallons of crude oil, departed Valdez. Shortly after midnight, Hazelwood was in his stateroom when the *Exxon Valdez* struck the reef. Eleven million gallons of oil subsequently gushed from a rip in its hull, making it the worst oil spill in U.S. history. A significant result of the incident was a dramatic tightening of regulations controlling the consumption of alcohol by those who operate commercial vessels.

Currently, U.S. Coast Guard regulations do not prohibit the presence or consumption of alcohol aboard commercial vessels, but they consider a person with a blood alcohol concentration of greater than or equal to 0.040 percent to be legally impaired and subject to removal and prosecution.[4]

Early on at CTI, individual captains were given discretion over the presence and consumption of alcohol on the company's vessels. Some were strict and permitted absolutely no drinking, while others allowed a few drinks after the work at hand was done. In 1995, because of the *Exxon Valdez* and new Coast Guard regulations, the policy was tightened to zero tolerance, and in the words of George Collazo, the company's port captain, the policy was "ruthlessly enforced." Today each crewman signs a contract stating that he will not drink during the voyage, not only when aboard ship, but even in ports that may be visited. Crew call for vessels is six hours before sailing time, in part to make sure that no one is impaired by alcohol (or drugs). It is understood that if a crewmember is caught drinking on the way to Alaska, he will be fired at the first port and given an airline ticket back to Seattle, the cost of which is deducted from his pay. A flight from Dutch Harbor to Seattle can cost $2,000. If a crewmember is caught drinking on the return to Seattle, he is fired immediately upon the vessel's arrival. CTI employs some alcoholics, and ironically, they appreciate the zero-tolerance policy for the simple reason that they want to stop drinking.

While alcohol on board was common for much of the history of the Aleutian trade, it is now more a symbol of a bygone era.

While the Magnuson Act (1976) excluded foreign fishing vessels from U.S. coastal waters, the market for frozen Alaska seafood continues to be dominated by Asian buyers. In the photo above, a Japanese tramp freighter (right) takes frozen cargo from a catcher-processor vessel (unseen, far right). The tramper is loading most of the cargo into her own hold, while giving the Western Pioneer vessel *Sculpin* an occasional pallet load. This is a common cargo-transfer practice in the Aleutian Islands area.

CHAPTER 8

Changing the Rules:
The Magnuson Act Opens a New Frontier

JAPANESE HIGH-SEAS VESSELS BEGAN fishing in the eastern Bering Sea in 1930 and, as noted previously, re-entered the fisheries during the postwar period beginning in 1954. They were joined by the Soviets in 1958 and the Koreans in 1967. By 1968, these nations combined were annually catching more than a million metric tons of fish—mostly pollock—in the eastern Bering Sea and Aleutian Islands region. Their effort peaked in 1972, when they caught nearly 2.4 million metric tons, of which more than 80 percent was pollock.[1] Little thought was given to the conservation of the resource.

Senator Warren Magnuson

THE UNITED STATES CLAIMS A 200-MILE LIMIT

The issue of foreign fishermen operating in U.S. coastal waters began coming to a head in 1970. On the East Coast, hundreds of commercial fishermen petitioned the government to extend the U.S. fishing boundary from 12 miles to 200 miles.[2] On the West Coast, scores of American as well as Canadian fishermen announced the tying up of their boats to protest the foreign "invasion" of their fishing grounds.[3]

Unilaterally claiming a 200-mile exclusive fishery zone was at that time a controversial proposal with little support from the U.S. government. It was also not a new idea. As a result of treaty negotiations in the fall of 1954, Peru, Ecuador, and Chile had each claimed exclusive fishing rights for a

distance of 200 miles from their shores.[4] It was the official U.S. policy, however, to assert the right of U.S. citizens to fish on the high seas outside the three-mile limit of all coastal nations, including those in South America. In 1955, the Peruvian and Ecuadorian governments began seizing and fining U.S. tuna boats that were caught fishing within their 200-mile zones. Though some considered this to be an act of piracy, the U.S. State Department didn't want to disturb the international status quo regarding territorial waters by proclaiming its own 200-mile limit. It was the government's policy to simply file a protest with the offending government and to reimburse the tuna fishermen for their losses.[5] For their part, the U.S. Navy and Air Force were concerned that a U.S. claim of a 200-mile coastal zone might provoke similar claims by other nations and inhibit the U.S. military's ability to operate in coastal areas.[6]

Led by Senators Warren Magnuson (D-Wash.), Edward Kennedy (D-Mass.), and E. L. Bartlett (D-Alaska), Congress extended U.S. fisheries jurisdiction to 12 miles in 1966. This was a start, but it wasn't enough. The 12-mile limit hindered, but did not curtail, the foreign fishing effort off the U.S. coasts.[7]

The issue of extending U.S. fisheries jurisdiction beyond 12 miles was about conservation as well as economic opportunity. As Hiroshi Kasahara, a University of Washington College of Fisheries professor, pointed out, "Those [foreign] fleets are simply clobbering our stocks out there. If we don't find the answer for forcing fishing conservation, it isn't only going to hurt our harvesting fish we pursue now, but there won't be anything left when we reach the point of development where we can use those stocks in our industry."[8]

Marine Digest reported that Alaska Governor William Egan thought imposing a 200-mile limit was not the answer, but he hoped the United Nations Conference on the Law of the Sea scheduled for 1973 might arrive at a solution.[9] It did not.

The champion of the legislative effort to extend the boundary of U.S. coastal waters to 200 miles was Senator Magnuson. His greatest ally was Alaska Senator Ted Stevens (R). The magnitude of the foreign fishing effort in Alaska's coastal waters was alarming. In early 1974, Senator Stevens reported that government officials had counted 106 Soviet and 72 Japanese vessels fishing off Alaska's coast, a record number.[10] Their efforts were concentrated on catching pollock, a species that was at that time almost completely ignored by the U.S. fishing industry.

Senator Magnuson introduced 200-mile limit legislation (S. 961) in the fall of 1975. By that time, fully 15 nations had proclaimed their own 200-mile limits.[11] Yet the bill was controversial. It was, as historically had been the case, opposed by the State Department and the Navy and Air Force. Even Senator Stevens's fellow senator from Alaska, Democrat Mike Gravel, did not support the legislation. Gravel argued, according to the *Washington Post*, that "foreign overfishing is being reduced, and can likely be further reduced, by enforcement of international agreements already in place and by the prompt negotiation of further agreements."[12] President Ford favored a 200-mile limit, but one achieved through negotiation with other nations, not by unilateral legislation.[13]

It was a close vote, but what became known as the Magnuson Fishery Conservation and Management Act (later reauthorized as the Magnuson-Stevens Fishery Conservation and Management Act) became law on April 13, 1976.[14]

The legislation went into effect on March 1, 1977, and was a turning point for the beleaguered American fisheries. George Rogers, considered by many to be the dean of Alaska economists, said that the Magnuson Act "opened up a new frontier for Alaska."[15] "Americanizing" the fisheries of the Bering Sea, however, was a slow and uncertain process. One

issue was the sheer magnitude of the fishery. The U.S. fishing industry had nothing to match the foreign fleet's harvesting and processing capability. Markets for groundfish, as well, were uncertain. And there was also the issue of transportation. Clem Tillion, chairman of the federal North Pacific Fishery Management Council, stated that transportation costs were "absolutely the controlling factor on developing the Alaska groundfish fishery."[16] Everyone was aware that the Aleutian Islands area lacked the transportation infrastructure—such as docks and cold storage facilities—that would be necessary to fully Americanize the region's fisheries. In a 1974 address to the Transportation Club of Seattle, Charles Hiltzheimer, a vice president at Sea-Land Service, pointed out the need for central locations for the consolidation of fishery products, adding that carriers could not continue to operate "a multi-stop bus service up and down the Aleutian Chain."[17] The interim solution while foreign fishing operations were phased out was joint ventures, with American catcher boats—often crab boats retrofitted with trawl gear—delivering pollock and cod to foreign processing ships, with the final product being marketed worldwide.

The first U.S. post-Magnuson Act effort to process Bering Sea groundfish was during the winter of 1979-1980. Icicle Seafoods and the New England Fish Co. began processing and freezing Pacific cod at Dutch Harbor. Icicle's was a makeshift operation aboard the *Bering Star*, a barge equipped to process and freeze salmon and crab. The cod were purchased from three small crab boats that were outfitted with longline gear. Aboard the *Bering Star*, equipment designed to head and gut salmon was used to do the same with Pacific cod. The market for the frozen product was in Norway, where it would undergo further processing. A Dutch tramp freighter was contracted to transport the product. Because weather constrained the fishing effort, filling the tramper's holds took far longer than anticipated, and when the vessel finally departed, it was only partially loaded.[18]

Business historian Alfred Chandler in 1980 called the transportation problem facing shore-based groundfish processors in the Bering Sea "almost insurmountable."[19] The same year, *Pacific Fishing* pointed out that it cost seven cents per pound to transport Atlantic cod from Iceland to U.S.

Loading frozen cargo into *Coastal Navigator*'s "hatchsquare" in 2011. Compare this photo with the photos from the 1980s on the following page. Over the past 15 years, ensuring that cargo is not damaged en route has been of paramount importance. To protect it during the long, often rough voyage to Seattle, frozen cargo stored in the hatchsquare is carefully sheathed in layers of cardboard, plastic, and plywood.

East Coast markets, which was about eight cents less than it would cost to ship Pacific cod from Alaska.[20] Unlike king crab, which by this time had attained luxury-food status and could bear relatively high transportation costs, cod was a commodity item, and every cent counted.

As well as enabling conservation, rational management, and the potential Americanization of U.S. coastal fisheries, the Magnuson Act broadened the definition of a fishing vessel such that there was no doubt Western Pioneer's vessels fit the category and were exempt from Coast Guard inspection requirements. A fishing vessel was "any vessel, boat, ship, or other craft which is used for, equipped to be used for, or of a type which is normally used for—fishing; or aiding or assisting one or more vessels at sea in the performance of any activity relating to fishing, including, but not limited to, preparation, supply, storage, refrigeration, transportation, or processing."[21]

FROZEN FOODS: AN EXPANDING MARKET FOR COD AND POLLOCK

The domestic market for groundfish was also growing, in large part because of a change in the national attitude toward fish, which was seen as being more nutritious and having fewer calories than red meat.

The rapid growth of fast-food chains and restaurant franchises that specialized in seafood was the most

important factor. McDonald's first served its popular Fillet-O-Fish sandwich in 1962. The product was developed to cater to Catholics on Fridays, a day when many of that faith abstained from eating meat and poultry. The sandwich was initially made with halibut, but halibut was deemed too expensive and was quickly replaced with cod and, later, pollock.[22] Two fast-food chains that specialized in seafood, Red Lobster and Skippers Seafood & Chowder House, began business in 1969. In 1980, fast-food restaurants accounted for two-thirds to three-fourths of all groundfish portions sold in the United States.[23]

Home consumption accounted for most of the remainder. During the postwar years, freezers became increasingly common in U.S. homes, and frozen food began to supplant the traditional canned fare. Seafood marketers targeted American housewives, and by the mid 1960s, a wide variety of attractively packaged frozen seafood products was available.[24]

The growth in domestic demand for groundfish would not be felt in Alaska for a number of years. Though the cost of Atlantic cod (*Gadus morhua*) increased dramatically in the early 1970s, and there were signs that stocks of the popular fish might be stressed, there seemed to be no shortage of imports from Canada and Iceland. As late as 1980, Atlantic cod was even being exported to Alaska. Regarding pollock, very low labor costs allowed the Koreans to catch and freeze the fish aboard ships in the eastern Bering Sea, reprocess them in Korea, and export the finished product to the United States, where it was used—unknown to most American consumers—as a lower-cost substitute for cod.[25]

Seafood products from the Bering Sea were also exported, particularly to Japan, which was principally interested in Tanner crab. Dutch Harbor is opportunely located for service to Japan because vessels traveling the Great Circle Route between the U.S. Pacific Northwest and the Far East transit Unimak Pass, which is only about 70 miles from Dutch Harbor. By 1980, both Sea-Land Service and American President Lines (APL) were offering service from Dutch Harbor to Japan. Sea-Land's service was every three weeks. In the spring of 1980, APL completed a new dock and container terminal at Dutch Harbor and offered the service—during the fishing season—on a weekly schedule. Transit time

was six days. To facilitate adequate cargo volume, APL also offered feeder barge service to Dutch Harbor from Beaver Inlet, King Cove, and Cold Bay.[26]

TRIDENT SEAFOODS: PIONEER SHORE-BASED GROUNDFISH PROCESSOR

There were some 13 floating crab processors based at Akutan in 1981, the year Trident Seafoods began construction of the first shore-based plant in the Aleutian Islands area designed to include the processing of groundfish. At 47,800 square feet, the Akutan plant was a world-class, state-of-the-art facility that was—in addition to processing other species—capable of processing 600,000 pounds of round cod per day.[a] Overall, the plant was a strong and concrete expression of confidence in the region's fisheries future. Chuck Bundrant, the founder of Trident, was no stranger to the Alaska seafood industry. He got his start in 1973 with the 135-foot vessel *Billikin*, the first Alaska vessel to catch, cook, and freeze king crab. Bundrant knew that breaking into the groundfish business would be hard work and might not be profitable.[27]

Trident's groundfish operation was not designed to provide frozen products to the domestic market. Harking back to bygone years, the operation cut its teeth salting cod for the traditional markets in Europe, northern South America, and the Caribbean.[b] Between June 1, 1982, and May 31, 1983, Trident purchased 35.4 million pounds of codfish.[28] The ambitious company planned to expand operations to include freezing cod fillets for the domestic market, and it had received a $9.4 million loan from the federal government to do so. Unfortunately, on June 9, 1983, Trident's plant was destroyed by a fire. The company was undeterred, and rebuilding commenced in January 1984. The following August, Trident began producing 15-pound "shatterpacks" of frozen cod and pollock fillets.[29] Salting fish would be left to others.

---

a The establishment of the groundfish operation was fostered by an $800,000 federal (Saltonstall-Kennedy) grant.

b In 1982, Western Pioneer's *Dolphin* was transporting a heavy load of salt to the operation when it encountered severe icing conditions. Taylor Campbell, the vessel's first mate, said the cargo made the situation somewhat safer. He credited the low center of gravity provided by the "supersacks," stowed three high in both lower holds, with offsetting substantially the negative effect on stability of the weight of the ice that had built up on the *Dolphin*'s superstructure.

Western Pioneer vessel *Sculpin*, laden with deck cargo in the 1980s. Note the articulated hydraulic cranes.

Industry Briefs, 1980-1985

A SEAFOOD SLUMP AT DUTCH HARBOR

The expansion of the shore-based industry to include groundfish processing was an important diversification in the region's economy, and it came at a fitting time: the Bering Sea king crab population had crashed in 1979, and crab processors were pulling out of the area. At Dutch Harbor, only three processing plants operated during the summer of 1983. Citing declining cargo and high operating costs, cargo carriers reduced service to the region. After years of prosperity, Dutch Harbor found itself in a profound economic slump, and people looked to groundfish processing as a possible salvation.[30]

ALASKA MARINE SHIPPING AND ALEUT ALASKA SHIPPING LEAVE THE TRADE

Alaska Marine Shipping and its partner, Aleut Alaska Shipping, went out of business in 1982.[c] Agafon Krukoff, president of the Aleut Corporation, said the business had

been a losing proposition. "No matter what our revenues were, we were never able to cut operating costs sufficiently to show a profit," he said.[31]

One of the venture's problems was self-inflicted, because it involved changes that the carrier had made to the *Pribilof*. Despite considerable advice against doing so, the corporation had spent something like a million dollars installing a large self-propelled crane on its deck, mostly to lift containers. But the crane and the engine that powered it took up an inordinate amount of potentially revenue-producing deck space, leaving room for only six 20-foot containers. And many of the locations served by the *Pribilof* had no way of efficiently handling containers once they were offloaded. The crane's location on deck was also problematic: it could service only the No. 2 hatch.

A second problem was that Alaska Marine Shipping's lease on the dock/warehouse facility on the Lake Washington Ship Canal was not renewed. Suitable replacement space was scarce, and the company was forced to move to an almost unworkable location near the Duwamish River, where the dock, which was three miles from the warehouse, was so small that the *Pribilof* didn't even fit alongside. Before going out of business, Alaska Marine Shipping did manage to work a

---

c   The principals of Alaska Marine Shipping went into providing a tugboat service in Puget Sound and operating a tug-and-barge freight service.

Western Pioneer freighter *Marlin* in the 1980s. The *Marlin* was converted into a freighter from the 156-foot version of yard oilers (YOs) constructed by the Navy. The five additional YOs that Western Pioneer converted into freighters were all 174-footers.

couple of voyages with both the *Aleut Packer* and *Snowbird*.[32]

After the company's demise, the *Pribilof* was initially leased to a seafood company that converted it into a processor, and then sold outright. The *Snowbird* was likewise initially leased to a seafood processor, then sold outright to an individual who converted it back to king crab fishing. The *Aleut Packer* was sold to Western Pioneer, which despite the slump was operating five vessels in the region and had pretty much a monopoly on the break-bulk freight business.[33]

COMMERCIAL FUR SEALING ENDS IN THE PRIBILOFS

Western Pioneer also serviced the Pribilof Islands, carrying general cargo north, and fur seal skins and sealburger south.[34] But change was afoot in the islands, which for nearly two centuries had been dependent upon the harvest of fur seals. Due in large part to pressure from conservationists, Congress in 1983 enacted legislation to terminate federal management of the islands and end the fur seal harvest.[35] No longer would the people there be able to count on the government program for their livelihoods. The islands were in close proximity to rich fishing grounds that were in the process of being Americanized, so development of a fish-

processing industry seemed a possibility. But before this could happen, suitable harbors would have to be constructed. Remoteness, severe geography, and extremely harsh weather guaranteed this to be an expensive proposition. The last commercial fur seal hunt in the Pribilofs took place on St. Paul Island in 1985.

COASTAL TRANSPORTATION AND SUNMAR SHIPPING ENTER THE ALEUTIAN TRADE

Coastal Transportation entered the Aleutian trade in 1984 with one vessel. Sunmar Shipping entered the trade in 1986 with two vessels. (See Chapter 9.)

• • •

Western Pioneer Diversifies

In 1981, Amigo and Max Soriano bought out the rest of the family and a couple of years later began diversifying Western Pioneer.[36] In 1983, they entered the fuel distribution and sales business with the formation of the subsidiary Delta Western, which served ships, airplanes, and motor

Western Pioneer's vessels were moving an increasing amount of cargo into and out of Dutch Harbor, but operations there were hamstrung because the company lacked a local terminal. Western Pioneer had been utilizing its customers' docks to load cargo, an arrangement that worked fine when the cargo belonged to the customer, but was awkward when the cargo was for someone else. This situation was rectified in November 1986, when Western Pioneer purchased a tract of land near the Dutch Harbor spit that included several docks and warehouses. These facilities were soon expanded and upgraded, and a number of reefer vans were brought in to hold frozen product. (At one point, there were about two dozen reefer vans on the property.) Included in the land purchase was a general store that eventually became the above-mentioned Alaska Ship Supply, a company that has flourished with the growth of Dutch Harbor.[38]

On three of the company's ships (*Sculpin*, *Marlin*, and *Tarpon*), Amigo replaced the traditional mast and boom ("yard-and-stay") rigging with articulated hydraulic "Husky" cranes mounted on deck. Although a tremendous amount of freight was moved with them, they were not really the best technology. The cranes were not as easy to operate as booms. Each machine required two men, one to "drive" and the other to tend hatches. Moreover, they took up space on deck, they could not lift heavy loads, and the diesel-powered version was very noisy.[d][39] In about 1987, Western Pioneer leased the 180-foot *Denali* to augment its fleet. The vessel came fitted with traditional mast and boom rigging, which worked so efficiently that it convinced Western Pioneer to abandon refitting its vessels with cranes.

Beginning in 1987, Western Pioneer leased the *Denali*. She began life as the *F. E. Lovejoy* in 1946, hauling newsprint between ports in British Columbia and Puget Sound. As she was never meant for the open sea, let alone the treacherous Gulf of Alaska and Bering Sea, her wooden wheelhouse and crew accommodations had no passageways connecting them. To go anywhere, crewmembers were forced to brave the open, windswept deck.

vehicles with a system of fueling stations that included facilities at Dutch Harbor, St. Paul, and St. George. Western Pioneer also branched into selling marine supplies with its purchase of Seattle Ship Supply and Gourock Trawls and the establishment of Alaska Ship Supply.[37] The maritime transportation component of Western Pioneer's portfolio would continue to grow, but at the same time, it would gradually become a secondary component of the business.

When Amigo and Max Soriano took over the business, Western Pioneer was operating six small freighters (in order of acquisition: *Marlin*, *Tarpon*, *Sculpin*, *Dolphin*, *Bowfin*, and *Capelin*), each a converted YO. Communication with the ships, particularly during the day, was hit-or-miss via single sideband (SSB) radio. SSB radio waves travel best after dark, so the company established a schedule by which an employee came to the Seattle-area office at a specified time each night and attempted to contact each of the vessels to get their location, weather, estimated time of arrival, and other pertinent information.

d   The *"Little" Dolphin* and the *Marlin* were equipped with a single electric crane, while the *Tarpon* and *Sculpin* had two diesel cranes. The *Aleut Packer* had a single electric crane as well as booms.

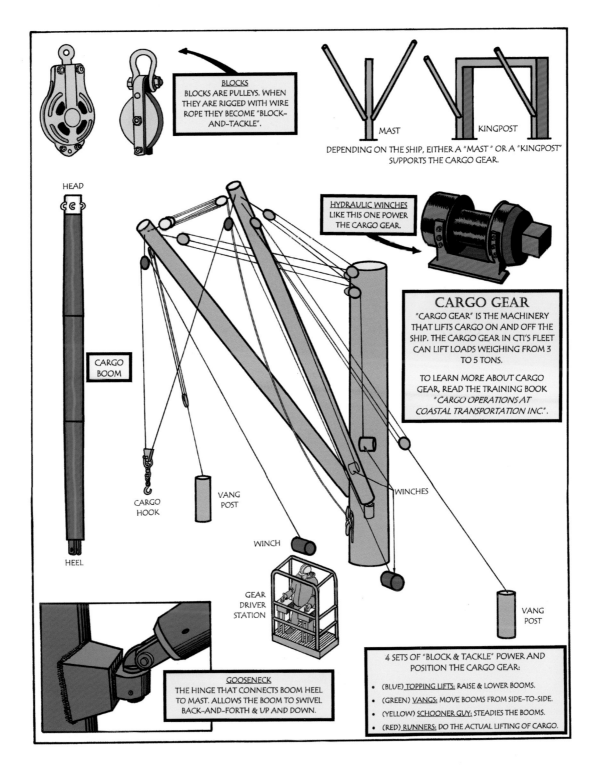

BLOCKS
BLOCKS ARE PULLEYS. WHEN THEY ARE RIGGED WITH WIRE ROPE THEY BECOME "BLOCK-AND-TACKLE".

MAST   KINGPOST

DEPENDING ON THE SHIP, EITHER A "MAST" OR A "KINGPOST" SUPPORTS THE CARGO GEAR.

HEAD

HYDRAULIC WINCHES LIKE THIS ONE POWER THE CARGO GEAR.

CARGO BOOM

CARGO GEAR

"CARGO GEAR" IS THE MACHINERY THAT LIFTS CARGO ON AND OFF THE SHIP. THE CARGO GEAR IN CTI'S FLEET CAN LIFT LOADS WEIGHING FROM 3 TO 5 TONS.

TO LEARN MORE ABOUT CARGO GEAR, READ THE TRAINING BOOK "CARGO OPERATIONS AT COASTAL TRANSPORTATION INC.".

CARGO HOOK

VANG POST

WINCHES

HEEL

WINCH

GEAR DRIVER STATION

VANG POST

GOOSENECK
THE HINGE THAT CONNECTS BOOM HEEL TO MAST. ALLOWS THE BOOM TO SWIVEL BACK-AND-FORTH & UP AND DOWN.

4 SETS OF "BLOCK & TACKLE" POWER AND POSITION THE CARGO GEAR:

- (BLUE) TOPPING LIFTS: RAISE & LOWER BOOMS.
- (GREEN) VANGS: MOVE BOOMS FROM SIDE-TO-SIDE.
- (YELLOW) SCHOONER GUY: STEADIES THE BOOMS.
- (RED) RUNNERS: DO THE ACTUAL LIFTING OF CARGO.

Description of yard-and-stay cargo gear, from the Coastal Transportation training manual *Seamanship for Beginners.*

Peter Strong, standing
on the deck of his Alaska
salmon tender *Seldovia*
in the 1970s.

SELDOVIA   SELDOVIA

CHAPTER 9

New Guys on the Block:
Coastal Transportation and Sunmar Shipping

COASTAL TRANSPORTATION, INC.

Coastal Transportation, Inc. (CTI) was founded by Peter Strong, who grew up mostly in Seattle. Several summers of his youth were spent in Searsport, Maine, where his father, by profession an American history teacher at the University of Washington, worked seasonally as director of a small maritime museum. It was through his father that Strong developed his abiding sense of history and deep interest in maritime matters.

In 1972, after completing classes at a small maritime trade school housed aboard an old ship moored in the Lake Washington Ship Canal, Strong took a seasonal job as the engineer on the Petersburg, Alaska-based cannery tender *Decorah*. The boat showed its age and the pay wasn't especially lucrative, but overall it was a nice adventure for a young man with an interest in the sea. He wanted an operation of his own.

Over the following winter, with the help of money borrowed from a friend, Strong purchased the *Orient* for $15,000. The 90-foot vessel was a classic wood-hulled schooner, constructed in 1912 and powered by an aged Atlas diesel engine. The summers of 1973 and 1974 were spent tendering salmon in Southeast Alaska under contract with Pelican Cold Storage.

In the fall of 1974, Strong sold the *Orient* and purchased the *Seldovia*, a World War II-vintage 86-foot wood-hulled power scow that he used to tender salmon in Prince William Sound. Strong married his wife, Leslie, in 1976, and assisted by a deckhand, they operated the *Seldovia* for several years. The vessel, moored at Seattle's Fishermen's Terminal, was their first home. In 1980, he acquired the salmon tenders *Caleb Haley* and *Tonsina*, the services of which were contracted to

canneries in Alaska. The Strongs' first child, Elliot, was born in December 1980.

Having a child is what pushed Strong toward the freight business. He didn't want to raise Elliot on a boat, or be separated from his family during the fishing season. He needed to find another occupation, ideally one that involved boats and Alaska.

Opportunity, though very uncertain, presented itself in the 180-foot *Theresa Lee*. The former Army FS ("freighter, small") had been converted in the 1970s into a floating crab processor by the New England Fish Co., and had also been used to carry cargo between Seattle and Alaska. New England Fish was going through bankruptcy proceedings, and the vessel was up for sale. Strong, always alert to a good deal on a boat, purchased it for $180,000 in late 1983. He immediately offered to lease it to Amigo Soriano, but according to Soriano, the vessel wasn't suitable for the trade. Among the problems were hatches that were too big and cargo gear that was too light. Soriano declined the offer. There was nothing, however, to prevent Strong from forming a company of his own and competing with Western Pioneer in the Aleutian trade. Coastal Transportation was incorporated in early 1984, and the *Theresa Lee* was promptly renamed *Coastal Trader*. A captain and crew were hired to man her, and a salesman engaged to sell cargo space.

The *Coastal Trader*'s first voyage north departed Seattle on June 3, 1984, from the Peter Pan Seafoods dock on the north shore of the Seattle Ship Canal. She was loaded with typical seafood-related cargo: packaging material, salt, groceries, etc. Joel Stewart, who had previously operated cannery vessels and fished king crab in the Bering Sea, was

Captain Joel Stewart, looking down from the wheelhouse of the *Coastal Trader* in 1984.

captain. The trip was pretty uneventful, save a pneumatic system problem that prevented bridge control of the vessel's main engines.[1] The *Coastal Trader* returned to Seattle with her holds full of opilio crab.

It was a good time to enter the Aleutian trade as a small break-bulk operator. Despite the general slump in activity at Dutch Harbor, the opilio crab fishery was booming, with long seasons and huge catches. A large portion of the catch was processed aboard floating processors, which had limited storage capacity and were usually unloaded at sea. And the only direct competition for the floating processors' business was Western Pioneer. The demand for southbound cargo space was at times so great that Western Pioneer rationed it. This presented a major problem for the company's lower-tier customers, who sometimes had to cease processing operations because their storage area was full. Trident Seafoods—on its way to becoming the largest seafood processor in Alaska— was very supportive of CTI, and early on shipped enough cargo to help the new company get established.

Joel Stewart intermittently operated CTI vessels for five years. Obtaining southbound cargo in those years was largely a catch-as-catch-can affair. Some was prearranged through the company's Seattle office, but a considerable amount was the result of Stewart simply calling around to processors once he arrived in Dutch Harbor. The resourceful Stewart, a licensed scuba diver, once traded diving services—clearing a fouled propeller on a catcher/processor –in exchange for 200,000 pounds of frozen cargo to top off his load.[2]

SEA STORY NO. 2

Stewart recalled some harrowing times, the most serious being on the *Coastal Trader* during the winter of 1987 or 1988. The vessel was en route from Dutch Harbor to Seattle, laden with a cargo of frozen crab sections. One especially stormy night, the seas were 40 feet high and building, and the wind blowing a steady 80 knots and gusting to more than 100 knots. The ride was so violent that the crew wasn't aware a serious problem had developed.

At first light, they were alarmed to see that the *Coastal Trader*'s bow was riding low. Also, the temperature in the lower No. 1 hold had risen. Stewart turned the vessel to run with the seas in order to provide a calmer ride so the crew could determine what was going on. They found that a small section of deck plate beneath the anchor winch had rusted through. Under the continuous washing by the heavy seas, seawater had leaked in and found its way through the forepeak and into the hold below, where it filled the spaces between the boxes of crab.

The crew was successful at making a temporary repair, but the incident was too close for comfort; if the leaking had not been stopped in time, the vessel would have been lost. And the ordeal was not yet over even after the vessel was safely in Seattle; the lower No. 1 cargo hold now contained a solid block of ice and fish. Figuring out how to unload it was a job for the shore crew.

Compared to the vast amount of meteorological information that is readily available to mariners today, the marine weather forecasts that Stewart relied on during the 1980s left much to be desired. Like nearly every other mariner in the Gulf of Alaska or Bering Sea, Stewart depended on

The 180-foot *Coastal Trader* in Dutch Harbor on her maiden voyage in the summer of 1984. She started life in 1945 as U.S. Army vessel *FS-232*. She was renamed *Theresa Lee* and during the 1970s converted by the New England Fish Co. into a floating crab processor. The vessel was purchased in 1983 by Peter Strong, who converted her into a freighter and renamed her *Coastal Trader*. The *"Trader,"* as she was called, was a trim, reliable boat, and loved by her crews. She burned in a fire at sea in October 1997. The crew escaped unharmed.

CLOCKWISE FROM TOP LEFT:

The original *Coastal Nomad* (ex-*Biscayne Freeze*) on her maiden voyage to Alaska, August 2, 1985. Built by the famous Davie Shipbuilding of Lauzon, Quebec, she had the loveliest lines of any of Coastal Transportation's freighters. By the time she was acquired by Coastal Transportation, however, she had fallen on hard times in the Caribbean, as evidenced in part by the extensive rust.

Coastal Ranger in Unimak Pass, late 1990s/early 2000s. Infamous for rolling wickedly in even moderate seas, the *"Ranger"* had the dubious honor of being voted by CTI's mariners as the worst boat in the fleet. As Port Captain George Collazo, who was responsible for hiring those mariners, said, "The *Ranger* was a hole in the water I threw people into." Regardless, the *Coastal Ranger*, like all the ex-Navy YO (yard oiler) and ex-Army FS (freighter, small) hulls, was exceptionally tough, and kept a regular schedule through heavy seas that gave pause to captains on much larger vessels. Not one vessel operated by Coastal Transportation, Western Pioneer, or Sunmar Shipping ever sank. "Not for want of trying," added Collazo.

The *Coastal Voyager*, taken at the outset of her maiden voyage on May 15, 1987. She was a small Army freighter converted to the Alaska fish processor *Viceroy*, then to an Aleutian freighter. In CTI's early years, the company bought a new boat every year or two, and each boat had to be converted into an Aleutian freighter. Supervision and labor for the projects fell to the company's seamen, who grew skilled at everything from engine repair to steel construction. Nevertheless, there was never enough time to get everything done correctly before a boat had to go to sea to earn her keep. This was the case with *Coastal Voyager*'s wheelhouse. In this photo, the wheelhouse is about 10 feet shorter than in the adjoining photo, taken in 1994. The construction of a new, taller wheelhouse for the *Coastal Voyager* had to wait for a year. Until then, the captain stood atop the wheelhouse to land the vessel and to steer her through heavy traffic. (Note the throttle and rudder controls just inboard of the starboard running light.)

Coastal Transportation's *Coastal Voyager* in 1994. The *"Voyager"* led a charmed life at CTI, surviving twice being run aground. The second grounding—which occurred in the Aleutian Islands—ripped open her fuel tanks from the bow to the engine room bulkhead and flooded her lower forward hold. Though her rudder was torn off and both propellers were severely damaged, her captain brought her back over 40 miles to safe harbor in Unalaska by alternating power to the propellers. Upon arriving at Unalaska, the captain was promptly fired for drinking.

Peggy Dyson, the wife of a Kodiak crab fisherman, for weather information. Under contract with the National Weather Service, Dyson in 1974 began broadcasting the marine forecast—and sometimes personal messages—to those at sea from a marine-band (SSB) radio station (WBH-29) at her home. The broadcasts were daily, at 8:00 a.m. and 6:00 p.m. After Dyson read the forecast—Stewart recalled the dire tone of voice Dyson used when the forecast for an area was "Storm warnings! I repeat, storm warnings!"—vessels throughout the region called in to give their location and the local conditions. The information was used to help forecasters, but was also of great value to other vessels in the region. Dyson also relayed personal messages to vessels.[a] Peggy Dyson's service was discontinued in 1999 and replaced by recorded or, more recently, synthesized voice broadcasts of marine forecasts and weather over dedicated radio channels.

From the beginning, Strong focused on delivering the best service he could, with the company goal of being "the best provider of transportation services in our class by providing high-quality, dependable, on-time service to our customers."[3] CTI's business model was very simple: do what Western Pioneer did, but do it better. It is the nature of the business that there were always customers who were for some reason dissatisfied with Western Pioneer's service or scheduling. CTI sought them out and tried to offer something more satisfactory. CTI also endeavored to distinguish its business from that of Western Pioneer. Western Pioneer operated what was essentially a tramper service, coming and going as cargo loads dictated. CTI posted and adhered to a schedule that customers could plan around. In the parlance of mariners, his was a "liner service." Initially, Seattle departures were scheduled on an approximately monthly basis, which was all that CTI's one vessel could manage. Once Strong's fleet was large enough, he scheduled a departure from Seattle every Friday evening. The service is popular with customers because it allows them the entire workweek to deliver northbound cargo. Strong also strove to accommodate last-minute customers at all points along the route.

---

a   Angus Whyte, of Alaska Marine Charters, said that when weather conditions prevented him from contacting the company's vessels via SSB radio, he would phone Dyson to ask her to relay messages.

Leslie and Peter Strong at the dedication of Coastal Transportation's Seattle terminal, 1989.

Strong added vessels as quickly as he could manage. In 1985 he purchased the Canadian-built *Biscayne Freeze* at a federal government auction. The 240-foot vessel had been built specifically to transport frozen codfish on Canada's Atlantic Coast, but later earned her keep transporting marijuana from Colombia to the United States. The *Biscayne Freeze* was seized in 1982 by the U.S. Coast Guard and eventually forfeited to the U.S. government.[4] A provision of the Merchant Marine Act of 1920—the same act that requires all vessels transporting cargo (or passengers) between U.S. ports to be of U.S. registry—allows foreign-built vessels seized by federal officials for illegal activities in U.S. waters to be redocumented as U.S. flag vessels. The *Biscayne Freeze* was renamed *Coastal Nomad* and almost immediately entered service. At the time she was the largest ship in the Aleutian trade, with 45,000 cubic feet of refrigerated space and a large dead-weight capacity. The addition of the *Coastal Nomad* allowed CTI to expand its service to twice monthly.

To better accommodate its expanding operations, CTI moved that year to a dock at the former Maritime Shipyards, on the south shore of the Lake Washington Ship Canal just west of Fishermen's Terminal.

In 1986, Strong purchased the 178-foot *Mokuhana*. The vessel had been constructed in 1953 to haul sugar on the Sacramento River and was later converted into a crab processor. The *Mokuhana* wasn't particularly well-suited for the Aleutian trade. She had a shallow draft and a flat bottom, and was slow. Additionally, because of the manner in which her decks were arranged, her deadweight capacity was low. But Strong needed additional capacity, and the *Mokuhana* had 40,000 cubic feet of refrigerated space and was available at a reasonable price. The vessel was renamed *Coastal Pilot* and promptly put into service.

In 1987, CTI added the *Coastal Voyager* to its fleet. Formerly the *Viceroy*, she was, like the *Coastal Trader*, built for the Army as an FS and later converted to process crab in Alaska. With a fleet of four vessels, CTI began offering weekly departures from Seattle to the Aleutian Islands area.

The demand for cargo space seemed to warrant an even larger fleet. More efficient terminal arrangements were needed as well. It was a big gamble, but in 1988 Strong purchased a 14-acre tract of industrial-zoned land on the Seattle Ship Canal, near the southeast side of the Ballard

Bridge. The site had formerly been occupied by a plywood mill. The company's operations were moved to the new location in September 1989. Today, CTI's Seattle cargo terminal can accommodate vessels up to 400 feet in length and 20 feet in draft. Importantly, the terminal is served by a spur of the Burlington Northern Santa Fe (BNSF) Railway, which provides direct, efficient distribution of seafood products to all the continental United States.

The only yard oiler (YO) to become a part of CTI's fleet was the *Coastal Ranger* (ex-*Double Star*), which was added in 1990.

Peter Strong refers to CTI's first five vessels as being among the first generation of Aleutian freighters. They were not as large and capable as the vessels that entered the service later but, nevertheless, did the job. All were in constant need of upgrade and repair. Joel Stewart said that Strong put "money into the ships as he could, and always listened to our safety concerns, and fixed problems as we reported them."[5] On average, the vessels in the first-generation fleet remained in the Aleutian trade for 14 years.

SUNMAR SHIPPING CO., INC.

In 1985, six transportation companies maintained regular service to Dutch Harbor. Sea-Land Service and American President Lines provided container-ship service, while Northland Services and Foss Alaska Line used tugboats towing barges to transport containers and deck cargo. Only Western Pioneer and the fledgling Coastal Transportation provided break-bulk cargo service.[6] In June of that year, American President Lines, likely sensing a substantial increase in commerce between the Aleutian Islands area and the Far East, announced that it would construct "the most modern, best equipped marine facility of its kind in the Aleutian Islands and Bering Sea area" at Dutch Harbor. The terminal would include a 300-foot dock and container lifts.[7]

The following year (1986), the Seattle-based Sunmar Shipping Co. began regular—though not scheduled—service to Dutch Harbor with two vessels, the *Sunmar Sea* and *Sunmar Sky*.[8] Sunmar was an independent shipping company that specialized in the ocean transportation of break-bulk refrigerated cargoes. It was formed in 1981 by

Hugh Thompson, construction supervisor for Coastal Transportation's Seattle terminal, 1989.

Hans W. Mauritzen and his longtime friend Olof Sundin. Both men had a wealth of experience in the industry. Mauritzen had been employed in executive capacities by a number of large shipping companies in Europe and the United States. Sundin was by profession a ship broker. The two initially brokered refrigerated cargo—principally Alaska seafood and Washington fruit destined for Europe—then became operators in the same market, chartering ships and finding cargo to fill them. Mauritzen described the work as both complicated and financially risky. In 1983, Mauritzen bought out Sundin.

Mauritzen recognized opportunity in the Aleutian Islands area, where there was a growing need for cargo capacity due to the ongoing Americanization of the groundfish fisheries. At that time, the region's two break-bulk carriers were working to maintain regular service to Dutch Harbor. Mauritzen saw a niche in doing what he characterized as "odd jobs," such as servicing at-sea processors, as well as providing service to Dutch Harbor and the Pribilof Islands. Though considerable, Sunmar's venture into the domestic (Alaska) service was a small part of the firm's overall business. Sunmar's dock/warehouse facilities in Seattle were located on the south shore of the Lake Washington Ship Canal, just east of CTI's current facility.

Sunmar's two Aleutian trade vessels were foreign-built.

Sunmar Sky (later the second CTI vessel to be named *Coastal Trader*) rides a large wave into the tiny harbor at St. Paul, in the Pribilof Islands. The harbor is entirely man-made and can be closed to vessels during periods of severe weather.

The 195-foot *Sunmar Sea* was originally constructed as a small bulk (sand) carrier in Sweden in 1956. The 257-foot *Sunmar Sky* was originally constructed in the Netherlands in 1963 as a dry cargo carrier. Both vessels had been seized by the U.S. Coast Guard after being caught smuggling drugs in U.S. waters and were acquired by Sunmar at a U.S. government auction. They were described by Mauritzen as "wrecks," but they had value: as with CTI's *Coastal Nomad*, a provision of the Merchant Marine Act of 1920 provided for their redocumentation as U.S. flag vessels.

The *Sunmar Sea* was purchased in Norfolk, Virginia, and in 1985 underwent a $1.8 million radical rebuild and renovation at the Marco Marine shipyard in Seattle. Upon completion of the work, the *Sunmar Sea* was basically all new forward of its wheelhouse. It was fitted with a bulbous bow to increase fuel efficiency and a bow thruster to increase maneuverability.

The *Sunmar Sky* was purchased in Savannah, Georgia, and delivered by a company crew to the Hyundai Mipo shipyard in Korea for renovation and a rebuild that was even more radical than that of the *Sunmar Sea*. This was the first rebuild of a reflagged vessel in a foreign shipyard, and it was important to ensure that there were no changes made that would jeopardize the vessel's U.S. registry. When the *Sunmar Sky* left the yard, its wheelhouse and everything forward of it was new. Additionally, it was fitted with an OmniThruster, a type of bow thruster that could rotate 360 degrees and actually propel the vessel, although slowly, in any direction. The total cost of the work done in Korea was $800,000, about

Sunmar Sky (later *Coastal Trader*) between an anchored Japanese tramp freighter (left) and an American fishing boat (right). Probably early 1990s.

half of what it would have cost in a U.S. shipyard.

Upon completion of their rebuilds, the *Sunmar Sea* and *Sunmar Sky*, although a bit slow, were basically state-of-the-art and functionally new refrigerated vessels. They were a large departure from the YO conversions that made up most of the Aleutian trade fleet.

In 1992, Sunmar added a third vessel, the *Sunmar Star*, to its Aleutian trade fleet. The 247-foot vessel had been constructed in Denmark in 1972 as a small container ship and was rated at 82 TEU, meaning it was capable of carrying the equivalent of 82 twenty-foot containers. Like the *Sunmar Sea* and *Sunmar Sky*, the *Sunmar Star* had been used to smuggle drugs and received U.S. documentation after being seized by the U.S. Coast Guard. The cost of the vessel, which required

little work, was about $600,000.[9]

Encouraged by the success of its three Aleutian trade vessels and optimistic about the future of the business, Sunmar purchased at auction three oil rig supply vessels. The company's plan was to rebuild them into three sister ships specifically for the Aleutian trade. Sunmar by now had enough experience in the trade to understand exactly what was needed in its vessels.

According to the company's plan, the midsection of each vessel would be cut out completely, and a much larger midsection custom fabricated and installed. The original forward (pilothouse) and rear (engine room) sections would be completely updated and renovated, and when everything was joined together, the vessels would be essentially new.

Using space above and below deck, each vessel would have a container capacity of 110 TEU. Adding to their versatility, the 70,000 cubic feet of hold capacity below deck was refrigerated and could accommodate either frozen break-bulk cargo or containers. Sunmar estimated that the vessels could make a round trip between Seattle and Dutch Harbor, including turnarounds, in 20 days, so with three vessels, weekly service could be maintained. The estimated total cost of putting the three sister ships on line was about $25 million. In the end, prudence demanded that Sunmar abandon the plan, and the three vessels that were to be its basis were sold off.

OFFICERS FOR THE SHIPS

Vessels can be built and maintained to the highest standards, but the competence of the individuals who man them is critical to efficient and safe operations. Amigo Soriano cultivated talent from his neighborhood in West Seattle to build a cadre of licensed ship's officers; Sunmar Shipping and CTI chose different options.

Sunmar found qualified officers for its ships with little difficulty by advertising positions nationally. Mauritzen considered chief engineers to be the most critical crew members because they understood the often complex and sometimes idiosyncratic systems that kept the ships operating. Every reasonable effort was made to retain experienced chief engineers. Though it may seem counterintuitive, captains were easier to replace than chief engineers, because a captain's basic job, navigating a ship between Seattle and the Aleutian Islands area, is relatively straightforward. Some captains lacked experience loading the greatly varied cargo that Sunmar's ships sometimes carried, so the company occasionally employed consultants, "freight captains," in Seattle to ensure that cargo was properly loaded and secured. This did not diminish the responsibility of ship captains, who always remain fully responsible for their vessels, including the cargo.

CTI initially found it easy to obtain licensed officers to man its vessels. The boom in Alaska's fisheries had drawn licensed officers to Seattle from all over the country, each hoping to land a lucrative job on a crabber or trawler. While waiting for their dream jobs, captains, mates, and engineers milled about the Seattle area and took work anywhere

they could, which was often at CTI. Ship's officers in the company in those years were often a mix of people on their way up and aged Alaska hands on their way out. The surplus of officers allowed CTI to keep wages low, which meant that there was more money available for management's primary goal of expanding the company's fleet. But there was a price to pay: some of those employed were, by any fairly rigorous standard, less than qualified for the demanding positions they held. On top of this, there were few standardized procedures for operating the company's ships. Managers at CTI allowed captains to operate them almost as individual fiefdoms, with each captain determining what was best for the ship under his command.[b] [10] The result of having marginally qualified individuals manning ships with few standardized procedures was a high accident rate, including groundings.

But that was a freewheeling time in the Aleutian trade. There seemed to be an almost endless supply of southbound cargo, Coast Guard regulations were few, and profits were high. Incidents such as groundings were viewed as part of the trade, just another cost of doing business. So long as no one was injured (or killed) or no oil was spilled, even the Coast Guard paid scant attention.

Industry Briefs, 1985-1990

SURIMI SAVES THE DAY

Salvation came to Dutch Harbor, or at least it began, in the shape of a product that few Americans were familiar with: surimi. Surimi is a fish paste made from the ground-up flesh of white-meated fish, and it has long been a staple of the Japanese diet. It is the basic ingredient in a variety of traditional products, including *kamaboko*, which is surimi to which starch and seasonings have been added that is then shaped into loaves and cooked by steaming. Sliced *kamaboko* is eaten with a dipping sauce. Surimi is also the basic ingredient of internationally marketed "seafood analogs": imitation crab, shrimp, and scallops.

b   Joel Stewart said that CTI in its early years "for the most part" had good crews that looked after each other and that there was a good sense of camaraderie aboard the company's vessels.

LEFT: *Coastal Sea* (ex-*Sunmar Sea*) in 2006 in Puget Sound. Her aft section came from the German gravel boat *Rodsand*, which was built in 1956. Everything forward of the wheelhouse was built new in 1985. This forward section was, however, built much wider than the aft section, and the transition between the two was an abrupt "step" in the hull. Between this flaw and the *Rodsand*'s antiquated engine, her maximum speed on a good day was barely nine knots. CTI acquired her in 1993 and smoothed her hull and replaced her engine. The result was that the *Coastal Sea* could easily maintain 12 knots, the speed of a typical Aleutian freighter. In an industry where maintaining a schedule is of paramount importance, the increased speed was critical.

RIGHT: *Coastal Trader* (ex-*Sunmar Sky*). The second vessel at CTI to bear the name *"Trader,"* she was acquired from Sunmar Shipping. Like the *Sunmar Sea*, the *"Sky"* was the pairing of an old engine room and superstructure, built in 1963, with a forward section built new in 1985. And, as with the *"Sea,"* the forward section was wider than the aft section. Not surprisingly, the *Coastal Trader* was slow until CTI faired out her hull and repowered her.

reason for locating the processing facilities at Dutch Harbor was that one of the most productive pollock grounds in the Bering Sea—an area known as the Horseshoe because of its shape—was located only 50 to 60 miles away. Trawlers could maximize time fishing and promptly deliver freshly caught fish to help ensure a first-class product.

PRIBILOF ISLANDS, HARBORLESS NO LONGER

Fishery-related development in the Pribilofs took a major step forward in the late 1980s, when federally assisted construction began on industrial boat harbors at St. George and St. Paul. The $60 million harbor at St. Paul, where the former fur seal processing plant was converted to process crab, was dedicated in the summer of 1990.[14] The $33 million harbor at St. George was first utilized in January 1991, when the floating processor *Galaxy* tied up to process crab.[15]

AT-SEA PROCESSORS

Shore-based processing and surimi were only one aspect of the growth of American processing capacity in the Bering Sea. Though the State of Alaska encouraged the development of a shore-based industry as a means of stabilizing the region's economy, at-sea processing came to dominate the fishery.

There are two types of at-sea processors: floating processing plants ("floaters") that process fish delivered by catcher vessels, and catcher/processor vessels that process their own catch.

The first U.S. catcher/processor in the post-Magnuson Act Alaska bottomfish industry was the 124-foot converted king crabber *Aleutian Mistress*, which was outfitted as a "factory longliner" with a highly automated system to catch (longline), fillet, and freeze primarily Pacific cod.[c] Its capacity was 20 to 30 thousand pounds of round fish per day. The vessel began operations in the Aleutian Islands area in November 1980.[16] Modern factory longliners operating in the Aleutian Islands area are generally 90 to 200 feet long.

Most bottomfish in the Aleutian Islands area, however, are caught by "factory trawlers" that catch fish (mostly

Leslie, Elliot, Linnea, Alicia, and Daniel Strong at Coastal Transportation's Seattle terminal in 1996.

In July 1985, Universal Seafoods, which had operated the crab-processing vessel *UniSea* at Dutch Harbor since 1975, purchased a shuttered plant (Pacific Pearl) and announced that it would equip it to manufacture surimi in a joint venture with the Japanese firm Nippon Suisan Kaisha, Ltd. The venture's plan was to spend some $10 million in renovating the plant to produce 10 million pounds of surimi annually. Of this, 80 percent would be exported to Japan and the remaining 20 percent would be shipped to Washington to be used to make imitation seafood products for U.S. markets.[11] Not long afterward, Universal Seafoods was purchased by Nippon Suisan Kaisha, and its name changed to UniSea. Its surimi-manufacturing plant was christened Great Land Seafoods.[12]

The Seattle-based Wards Cove Packing Co. entered into a similar joint venture with Taiyo Fisheries and Marubeni Corp. to form Alyeska Seafoods, which would construct and operate a surimi plant at Dutch Harbor.[13]

The surimi would be made from the flesh of the most abundant food fish in the Bering Sea: pollock. Part of the

---

c   The conversion of *Aleutian Mistress* from crabber to longliner was designed to be reversible, and took about three days either way.

CLOCKWISE FROM TOP LEFT:

Chief Engineer Mike Shull in the engine room of the *Coastal Navigator*.

Coastal Nomad Assistant Engineer (later Chief Engineer) Mark Ottak driving cargo gear at Chignik in 2008.

The fuels of choice for many a deckhand: cigarettes and energy drinks.

John Bunnell (right side up) and Jim Alongi (upside down) on the *Coastal Trader*'s bow, in 1987. Both men were engineers in the early Coastal Transportation fleet. Bunnell was typical of the adventurous individuals attracted to the trade. As a high school student in Seattle, he responded to a deckhand job offer posted on a telephone pole, which led to a summer exploring the South Pacific on a yacht. Just out of high school, he worked on a salmon tender in Alaska. In later adventures, Bunnell backpacked the 220-mile circumference of Unimak Island, motored up the Amazon River on his own boat, survived an insurrection on an Indonesian island, and built oil-exploration camps on Russia's Sakhalin Island.

pollock) in towed nets. Modern factory trawlers range in size from 220 feet to nearly 400 feet and are capable of catching and processing hundreds of tons of round fish per day. Some can store more than a thousand tons of frozen product. In 1991, the North Pacific Fishery Management Council, the policy-making body for federal fisheries off Alaska's coast, allocated fully 65 percent of the available groundfish harvest to the factory trawlers.[17]

Most of the services the factory vessels needed to keep operating—including storage and the transportation of supplies and product—were provided at Dutch Harbor. An increasing portion of these services came to be provided by Western Pioneer, which in a joint venture with Crowley Maritime (an Oakland, California-based tug and barge operation) in the spring of 1986 purchased Chevron's 13.5-million-gallon fuel terminal.[18]

NEW YORK INVESTORS BUY INTO WESTERN PIONEER

In 1988, Americanization of the Bering Sea groundfish fishery hit its first milestone: the U.S. capacity to catch groundfish was deemed sufficient to complete the Magnuson Act-mandated phaseout of foreign catcher vessels.[19] The employment of foreign vessels to process the catch was still necessary, but it too was quickly coming to an end.

At least some in the investment community must have believed that Western Pioneer was positioned to grow quickly or was worth more than its books showed, because

in December 1988, the Equitable Life Assurance Society of the United States and Lepercq, de Neuflize & Co., New York-based investment firms, together purchased a half interest in the company.[d] It was a leveraged buyout, done with borrowed money in expectation of quickly reselling the company or its assets. The buyout agreement included a provision stating that Amigo and Max Soriano were to remain on the company's board of directors as well as retain their respective positions as president and vice president/secretary-treasurer. As such, Amigo and Max Soriano continued to oversee the day-to-day operations of the firm.

Prior to the buyout, the wealth of those who had become the principal owners of Western Pioneer (Amigo and Max Soriano; Amigo's son Steve; and Gary Sergeant, the company's chief financial officer) had been largely tied up in the company. For them, the buyout provided a substantial infusion of cash.

They didn't keep it all for themselves, however. Western Pioneer had always considered itself a family-style operation, and it was company policy to distribute a bonus each Christmas to employees to show their appreciation and to share some of the year's profits. That year's Christmas bonus was one to remember: Amigo, Max, and Steve Soriano, as well as Gary Sergeant, each contributed a million dollars to form a $4 million pool of money that was divided among present and past employees who had helped make Western Pioneer what it was.

d   Lepercq, de Neuflize & Co. was a subsidiary of Lepercq, Inc.

Coastal Sea during a quiet moment at the dock in Atka, a small community in the Aleutian Islands.

CHAPTER 10

Congress the Facilitator:
The Aleutian Trade Act

CONGRESS IN 1984 WAS REWRITING TITLE 46 OF THE U.S. CODE, THE REGULATIONS THAT GOVERN SHIPPING. Title 46 was replete with exceptions for the fishing industry, and Congress wanted to remove them and set up separate laws for vessels that transported fish. In the process, Western Pioneer pointed out that their uninspected vessels had been carrying general cargo for a number of years. Congress, in response, decided to authorize the continuation of the practice for five years, with the understanding that Western Pioneer's vessels would be brought up to Coast Guard Certificate of Inspection standards.[1] The legislation was largely tailored to Western Pioneer's fleet, stating that a fish tender of not more than 500 gross tons that was "in operation, or contracted for purchase to be used as a vessel of this type, before July 1, 1984, may transport cargo to or from a place in Alaska not receiving weekly transportation from a port of the United States by an established water common carrier."[2] As written, the legislation precluded to a certain extent potential competition in the general cargo niche Western Pioneer had carved out for itself. Apparently the company counted on its special treatment being extended beyond the legislated January 1, 1990, expiration date, because no effort was initiated to bring the vessels being operated (all converted YOs) up to the standards necessary to receive a certificate of inspection. With no alternative transportation options available, politicians would find it very difficult to eliminate service to the substantial number of small ports that only Western Pioneer served.

In late 1989, as the end of Western Pioneer's general cargo exemption period approached, the company asked Congress for an extension. Western Pioneer, by this time, had done nothing to bring its converted YOs up to Coast Guard inspection standards, but it had added three vessels to the fleet. The *Sally J* (later renamed *Bluefin*), *Redfin*, and *Yellowfin* were all former oil rig service vessels ("mud boats") designed to transport supplies, especially drilling mud and drill pipe, to offshore oil rigs. It was the opinion of some that it would not be difficult to bring these three vessels up to Coast Guard inspection standards. The principal reason for the purchase of the former oil rig tenders, however, was that the economy of scale was superior to that of the YO fleet. Each of the vessels could carry more than twice the amount of freight that a converted YO could, but needed no additional crewmen.

Western Pioneer opposed being forced to operate Coast Guard–inspected vessels. It wanted the option to utilize uninspected vessels or, if it chose, to upgrade to meet inspection requirements. To avoid what Amigo Soriano called the "substantial and extremely expensive refitting" of the company's fleet, Western Pioneer needed a permanent exemption from the Coast Guard inspection requirements. It was expected that in the course of a general upgrading of the company's fleet, however, some vessels—likely the former oil rig tenders—would eventually be modified to meet Coast Guard inspection standards.

Large carriers, such as Sea-Land Service and especially Crowley Maritime, opposed the exemption basically because they wanted a segment of their competition eliminated. They argued that all carriers operating a line haul service (from Alaska to Seattle, for instance) should work under the same set of rules, that uninspected vessels be allowed to operate only within Alaska, and that uninspected vessels be restricted to serving ports that did not receive regular weekly water common carrier service. They suggested that companies not wanting to operate inspected vessels should have their cargo shipped from Seattle to Kodiak or Dutch Harbor on an inspected general cargo carrier such as Sea-Land, then load it on the uninspected vessels for delivery to those communities that had no regular weekly common carrier service.

Soriano responded that the big companies were "trying to drive us out of business," that being able to operate the line haul service to Dutch Harbor, with its high volume of freight, was essential for Western Pioneer's service to the small communities to be feasible.

Congress's response to this conflict among the shippers was to extend the exemption for one year, during which time the parties involved were expected to work things out among themselves and then come back to Congress with a proposed legislative solution.[3]

The sentiment in southwestern Alaska was strongly in favor of a permanent extension of the exemption. There was a lot of appreciation for what was termed the "mosquito fleet" that had developed the freight service to the Aleutian Islands area. In the words of an Unalaska city councilman, companies like Western Pioneer had "stuck with us, done a helluva job, and maintained low rates."

But Paul Fuhs, mayor of Unalaska, warned that some in Congress would argue that the exemption deadline was no surprise, and that safety was a factor. He said that the uninspected status of some vessels was a "sore spot" among many politicians. This was especially true after the sinking of the 162-foot factory trawler *Aleutian Enterprise* in March 1990. The waters of the Bering Sea were calm at the time of the sinking. Nine of the 31 persons aboard perished, including a federal fisheries observer. An article about the dangers inherent in fishing in the Bering Sea in the business publication *Fortune* noted that the uninspected vessel was "shoddy, the equipment inadequate, the crew poorly trained, and the captain was both inexperienced and under pressure from management." The *Aleutian Enterprise* wasn't a marginal operation; it was owned by the Arctic Alaska Fisheries Corp., the nation's largest fishing company.[4]

According to Amigo Soriano, Western Pioneer's vessels were "well-designed and maintained and our safety record is outstanding."[5] Indeed, despite some mishaps, in almost two decades of operation that involved hundreds of voyages along one of the most hazardous shipping routes in the world, the company had never lost a vessel or a crewman.

In the spring of 1990, the Unalaska City Council unanimously passed a resolution supporting "in the strongest possible terms" a proposed amendment to Title 46 of the U.S. Code that was provided by Western Pioneer, CTI, and Sunmar Shipping. The amendment was essentially the same as the 1984 legislated exemption without the sunset clause. An appendix to the resolution listed 39 Alaska communities that received cargo service by fish-tender vessels.[a][6] An accompanying Unalaska City Council position paper, "Authority for Fishing Industry Vessels to Carry General Cargo to Remote Communities in Alaska Should Be Continued," praised the shippers for the "safe, reliable, and competitive service to communities which have virtually no other transportation alternative."[7]

Of Alaska's congressional delegation, Representative Don Young was by far the most engaged in the Bering Sea transportation issue. Before he was elected to Congress, Young had for several years operated a riverboat on the Yukon River, so had some firsthand knowledge of commercial vessel operations.

On October 6, 1990, Young introduced the Aleutian Trade Act, which had been drafted by his office in consort with Western Pioneer, Coastal Transportation, and Sunmar Shipping.

Western Pioneer provided Young with a list of 20 vessels considered eligible for grandfathering under the proposed legislation. By ownership, they were:

Western Pioneer: *Marlin, Tarpon, Sculpin, Bowfin, Dolphin, Aleut Packer, Capelin, Sally J, Yellowfin, Redfin*
Arctic Alaska Seafoods: *Eastern Wind, Northern Wind*
Coastal Transportation: *Coastal Nomad, Coastal Ranger, Coastal Trader, Coastal Voyager, Mokuhana*
Sunmar: *Sunmar Sea, Sunmar Sky, Sunmar Star*

According to Young, the legislation was "designed to provide continued cargo service to remote communities in

---

a   Craig, Ketchikan, and Noyes Island (all in Southeast Alaska) were among those listed, as was Seward and "Washington Coast."

Alaska, while ensuring better safety standards for vessels operating in the Aleutian trade."[8] Young's claim was correct, but only in degree, for the legislation provided certain vessels operating in the Aleutian trade a broad exemption to the Commercial Fishing Industry Vessel Safety Act of 1988, which had been developed to help ensure safe operations.[9] Yet it engendered little controversy, and was incorporated into the Federal Maritime Commission authorization for fiscal year 1991, which was signed by President George H. W. Bush on November 16, 1990.[10]

The Aleutian Trade Act (ATA) defined a fish tender vessel as "a vessel that commercially supplies, stores, refrigerates, or transports fish, fish products, or materials directly related to fishing or the preparation of fish to or from a fishing, fish processing or fish tender vessel or a fish processing facility."

Under the ATA, special construction, safety, and manning regulations were to be developed by the U.S. Coast Guard for fish tender vessels of not more than 500 gross registered tons (GRT) operating in the Aleutian trade area.[b] In addition to the regulatory modifications, the ATA specifically permitted fish tender vessels to transport general cargo. The ATA also "grandfathered" 20 vessels (as noted above) that had operated

in the trade or had been purchased to be used in the trade. These vessels were given until January 1, 2003, to comply with the regulations that would be developed in accordance with the legislation. The ATA contains no sunset provision, and does not preclude additional fish tender vessels of not more than 500 GRT from entering the trade, but to do so, a vessel would have to comply immediately with ATA regulations.

At the very least, the ATA put a legal foundation beneath the small shipping lines that guaranteed they could continue to operate as they had for a dozen more years. But there was also a major uncertainty: would the regulations developed by the Coast Guard be onerous to the point of ultimately driving them out of business? The required procedure for promulgating new regulations is deliberative, inclusive, and usually lengthy. Largely because Congress provided only very general guidance in writing the ATA, the development of regulations for its implementation was somewhat complicated. CTI's general manager, Tim Shaffer, acted as an informal consultant to the Coast Guard while the regulations were being designed, and he worked to ensure that the final regulatory package was both practical and workable. The process of designing and formalizing the regulations took fully five years.

---

b   The Aleutian trade area is defined in the act as in Alaska west of 153 degrees west longitude and east of 172 degrees east longitude.

Coastal Transportation's *Coastal Sea* at dock in Alitak, on Kodiak Island, in 2006. In addition to the cargo holds, the weather deck is also piled high with cargo.

CHAPTER 11

The Aleutian Trade Fleet: Smaller and Better

IN ADDITION TO THE UNCERTAINTY OVER THE IMPLEMENTATION OF THE ALEUTIAN TRADE ACT, there was another, more fundamental problem that developed during the early 1990s: just being in the Aleutian trade was getting tougher. This was in part because environmental regulations were becoming stricter as a result of the *Exxon Valdez* oil spill in 1989, but mostly because the Aleutian Islands area fishing industry was evolving.

Most prominent among the changes was the dramatic shortening of Bering Sea groundfish seasons due to severe overcapitalization in the fishing fleet—more vessels were chasing roughly the same tonnage quota of fish. Where it had previously taken 10 months to catch the pollock quota, it now took only two. In addition to the increased seasonality of the trade, the pattern of how cargo was shipped from the Aleutian Islands area had changed. A considerably greater percentage was being shipped directly to the Far East and Europe on tramp freighters rather than being distributed through Seattle.

While there was still sufficient cargo to carry northbound, the reduced demand for southbound cargo capacity and the increasingly seasonal nature of the trade affected all modes of marine transport, including the container ships and the tug and barge operations. CTI, for example, was forced to lay off crews during the off-season. Many individuals left the company, which resulted in a high rate of crew turnover and a corresponding increased likelihood of accidents. The situation was similar at Western Pioneer, and it affected not only boat crews but dockworkers and office help as well. Larry Soriano said later that laying people off during the slow season wasn't an option because they would find employment elsewhere. He said Western Pioneer would make good money during the fishing season but "give it back" during the slower times.[1]

Paradoxically, there was one consequence of the fisheries slowdown that actually benefited the freight operators: reduced fishing resulted in a surplus of limited-tonnage officers. The surplus continued until about 1997, when a resurgence of oil field activity in the Gulf of Mexico increased the demand for their services and drove up wages substantially.[2]

In this tight market, CTI, Western Pioneer, and Sunmar Shipping, each eager to operate near capacity, attempted to poach each other's customers by reducing freight rates to what were at times nearly ruinous levels. Some customers, of course, were not beyond playing the carriers off against each other to get the best deal possible. The rate war that began about 1990 would last some dozen years.

CTI attempted to maintain profitability by increasing operational efficiency. The company's "wild west" days were over. In this competitive environment characterized by razor-thin margins, the avoidance of costly groundings and employee injuries—and the concomitant high insurance rates—became a serious priority at CTI. The company also worked to provide increasingly better service to its customers. Service, of course, begins with people, and Strong was fortunate to attract and retain a core group of very capable individuals. These include CTI's port captain, George Collazo, a graduate of the California Maritime Academy who has been with the company essentially since it began in 1984. Tim Shaffer, the company's general manager, joined in 1989. Four of CTI's current ship captains have been with the company for more than a decade.

Why would a competent holder of a master's license—a person who wouldn't generally have a difficult time finding work—choose to operate a small vessel in something of a backwater, albeit a dangerous one? Arthur Lynch, who has been a CTI captain since 1989, explained to me that if he were master of, say, a container ship on a trans-Pacific route, the standard operating procedure would be to take the helm only after a pilot had brought the vessel through the Strait of Juan de Fuca. In crossing the ocean, the policy would be to maintain a "CPA" (closest point of approach) of two to four miles from any other vessel, headland, etc. (The standard operational CPA at CTI is one mile.) Once he approached his destination port, a pilot would again take over. In his job with CTI, Lynch is in undisputed control of his vessel. He is able to do what he was trained to do and enjoys doing. There is a satisfaction in meeting the challenge, and the pay is competitive.

. . .

In 1992, the board of directors at Western Pioneer voted to remove Amigo Soriano from his position as president of the company. The reason given to the public for Amigo's removal was simply that he and the board were "not getting along."[3] Amigo, the patriarch of the Soriano family, was 77 years old at the time, and was replaced by his brother Max, who was a decade younger.[4] It is the opinion of some former employees that the company's shipping operations began to deteriorate when Amigo's operational expertise and leadership were lost.

The plan of the New York investors to quickly sell their interest in Western Pioneer didn't pan out, and in 1994, Soriano family members began gradually buying it back, a process that was completed in 1998.

. . .

In 1993, Sunmar Shipping began easing out of the Aleutian trade. The principal reason for the decision was that its owner, Hans Mauritzen, wanted to concentrate on his company's core businesses: transporting frozen seafood from factory trawlers operating in U.S. and Russian North Pacific waters to world markets; refueling fishing vessels at sea in the North Pacific and Russian Far East; and operating a regular container service between Puget Sound and the Russian Far East, which included a container terminal in Olympia.

There was also the issue of what Mauritzen termed *schedule integrity*. With just three small ships and a barge in his Aleutian trade operation, he was unable to reliably maintain a regular schedule between Seattle and the Aleutian Islands

area. Northbound cargo for Sunmar was only sporadically available, so the company's operation focused on carrying southbound cargo, which itself was sometimes scarce. Overall, it was an inherently less-than-efficient operation that was phased out to foster efficiency elsewhere in the firm. The first vessel taken out of service was the *Sunmar Sea*. She was purchased in the summer of 1993 by CTI and put into service the following year as the *Coastal Sea*. Her purchase was something of a gamble for CTI not just because of the cargo situation, but also because of the uncertainty over how the regulations being developed by the Coast Guard to implement the ATA would affect the industry. But largely because of Tim Shaffer's participation in the regulation-making process, Peter Strong had increasing confidence that the final ATA regulations would be reasonable.

. . .

It was perhaps a little premature, but early in 1995, Strong developed a one-page strategic plan for his company. The plan's title—"Vessel Acquisition Plan" (VAP)—stated its purpose. In it, Strong assumed that CTI would remain in the industry beyond the January 1, 2003, cutoff date for ATA-grandfathered vessels. His goal was to establish CTI as the dominant carrier in the Aleutian trade. The company would work to increase its customer base, and—as needed—obtain the vessels and develop the infrastructure to support expanded operations. Regarding the acquisition of vessels, he posed the questions of how much capacity would be ideal, and what the dimensions of the ideal vessel to serve the trade might be. Strong combed the trade publications and made a list of every vessel he thought might be suitable for the Aleutian trade. Those that offered the most promise were personally inspected by Strong or Shaffer, even if located on the East Coast.

. . .

The half-decade of uncertainty over the ATA ended in October 1995, when the Coast Guard published the final ATA regulations.[5] To the Coast Guard's credit, the regulations it developed succeeded at fostering safe operations in the

Coastal Transportation's dock in Dutch Harbor, with the Alyeska Seafoods wharf just across the passage to the inner harbor and the City of Unalaska in the background.

CLOCKWISE FROM TOP LEFT:

Coastal Navigator under way in Puget Sound in 2008. Two years later, she was lengthened by 40 feet. | Coastal Transportation's *Coastal Nomad* (formerly Western Pioneer's *Redfin*) in 2008. The *Coastal Nomad* is sister-ship to the *Coastal Progress* (formerly Western Pioneer's *Yellowfin*). Upon Coastal Transportation's purchase of the *Coastal Nomad* and the *Coastal Progress*, their hulls were modified and they were refitted with new main engines in a successful effort to reduce fuel consumption and make them profitable. | Captain Jason Sankey in the wheelhouse of the *Coastal Navigator* in 2008. Sankey entered the trade in 1993 as a deckhand. The demands of the trade require experienced captains. Superior navigation skills are a given; the true test of a deck officer in the Aleutian trade is the ability to rig, stow, and secure any kind of cargo quickly and safely. | *Coastal Progress* in 2007.

Aleutian trade without being unduly burdensome. Very importantly, the new rules provided a strong element of certainty regarding the regulatory environment in which the industry would operate for the foreseeable future.

To one not intimately familiar with the details of vessel design and construction, the regulatory changes resulting from the ATA are not noticeable, mostly having to do with matters such as the design and material used in the construction of fuel tanks; the height, design, and location of deck rails; and wiring methods and materials. Each of the regulations, however, is important, for even small mishaps at sea have a way of cascading into dangerous situations. Attention to detail is paramount.

To ensure compliance with the ATA, each vessel was required to pass an inspection by the American Bureau of Shipping or a similarly qualified entity at least once every two years. Vessels operating under the ATA are not required to obtain a Coast Guard Certificate of Inspection (COI), which involves a stricter and more comprehensive inspection. ATA-mandated vessel inspections began in 1996.

. . .

The first addition to CTI's fleet under the Vessel Acquisition Plan occurred in 1996. The 210-foot *Inge Frank* had been constructed in Germany 30 years earlier to carry dry and general cargo. She was flying the Belize "flag of convenience" in 1994, when she was seized after U.S. agents in Florida discovered secret compartments containing 4,300 pounds of cocaine.[6] The *Inge Frank* was subsequently forfeited to the U.S. government, redocumented as a U.S. flag vessel, acquired by CTI at auction, and renamed *Coastal Merchant*.

As it turned out, CTI's former competitors in Seattle were the company's biggest source of "new" vessels. The first of these was the *Sunmar Sea*, which was purchased from Sunmar Shipping in 1993 and renamed *Coastal Sea*. In 1997, Sunmar Shipping's *Sunmar Sky* was purchased and renamed *Coastal Trader*. In 1999, CTI increased the size of its fleet by purchasing the 195-foot *Sunmar Star* and the 178-foot *Northern Wind*. Both were ATA-grandfathered vessels. The *Sunmar Star* formerly belonged to Sunmar Shipping and was renamed *Coastal Venture*. The *Northern Wind* had been

constructed in 1991 by Arctic Alaska Seafoods specifically to service its western Alaska operations. (CTI could have purchased its ATA-grandfathered sister ship, *Eastern Wind*, as well, but Peter Strong felt that the *Northern Wind* was the better of the two.) Upon entering CTI's fleet, the *Northern Wind* was renamed *Coastal Navigator*.

After the addition of the *Coastal Venture* and the *Coastal Navigator* to its fleet, CTI increasingly sidelined the *Coastal Pilot* (formerly *Mokuhana*) in favor of larger ships. Despite her shortcomings, she had served well and hauled a lot of cargo. The *Coastal Pilot* was sold in 2008.

Owning ships is only one aspect of operating a shipping company. In order to reliably and efficiently load and discharge cargo, a certain amount of infrastructure—basically docks and warehouses—is essential. CTI's terminal in Seattle was (and is) a first-class facility, but the situation was different in Dutch Harbor, where Western Pioneer—the competition—had owned a dock and warehouses since 1986.

CTI vessels loading cargo from catcher/processors in Dutch Harbor usually did so while at anchor. An incident that occurred in late November 1997 removed that option during severe weather conditions—which is not infrequently the situation in a place that bills itself as the "Birthplace of the Winds."

The Japanese tramper *Kuroshima* had been lying at anchor in Dutch Harbor for about three weeks awaiting a cargo of frozen seafood, when she was struck by a powerful storm, with northerly winds gusting to 90 knots and high seas. The vessel broke anchor and ran hard aground. Two crewmen died and an estimated 39,000 gallons of fuel oil were released—the largest oil spill in Alaska since the *Exxon Valdez*. It took salvors more than three months to free the *Kuroshima*.[7]

To decrease the likelihood of similar incidents occurring, the U.S. Coast Guard established guidelines that restrict the transfer of cargo while at anchor in Dutch Harbor during severe weather conditions. As the owner of a dock, Western Pioneer clearly held an advantage over CTI in its ability to handle cargo.

A dock suitable for CTI's needs became available for lease after the 1997 fire that destroyed the East Point Seafoods processing plant. The facility's dock, which had been constructed in 1977 and was not damaged by the fire,

Coastal Merchant discharging cargo at the Coastal Transportation dock in Dutch Harbor in 2009.

was leased by CTI in 1999. It can accommodate vessels of the same size as those accommodated at the company's Seattle terminal. In true Dutch Harbor style, CTI parked forty-five 40-foot refrigerated vans ("Dutch Harbor Legos"—after the brightly colored toy building blocks) on the site. Still on the site today, these containers and others that have been added over the years have been stacked, disassembled, and restacked into sorting atriums, transit sheds, and warehouses. Even the CTI office is housed in modified shipping containers. The refrigerated units on the site are capable of holding some 3 million pounds of frozen product and offer considerable flexibility because cargo can be loaded or offloaded at any time. The dock was eventually purchased by CTI and is currently operated by a contractor. Despite its success with the versatile shipping containers, CTI's long-term goal for the facility is to construct conventional buildings.

. . .

Though Sunmar as a company had faded from the scene by the mid 1990s, its former ships hadn't. In the Aleutian trade there was still too much freight capacity for the freight available. CTI and Western Pioneer were competing for it, but there didn't seem to be room for them both.

Despite the decline in southbound cargo, Western Pioneer was still operating 10 ships in 1997. CTI was operating seven, but they were on average larger and provided better economies of scale—primarily because they were more fuel efficient—than those of Western Pioneer. Also, CTI owned its Seattle terminal. Western Pioneer rented its terminal at a very high monthly rate.

In some respects, the cargo decline may not have mattered to corporate Western Pioneer as much as it might have because of the company's successful diversification. In 1997, fully 70 percent of the $150 million in revenues generated by Western Pioneer was from fuel sales and distribution, a sector that was continuing to grow. The remainder was from an about-even split between retail sales and the operation of its cargo fleet.[8] Though there were definitely some good years among the bad, the real problem with the decline in shipping operations was that the situation seemed to be permanent.

Western Pioneer attempted to compensate for the decline in its traditional cargo market by bringing the *Bluefin*, *Redfin*, and *Yellowfin* up to Coast Guard inspection standards to allow for the expansion of service into transportation markets beyond those allowed under the Aleutian Trade Act. The endeavor was expensive and met with only modest success. The company considered but ultimately decided against bringing its remaining ATA-grandfathered vessels—all former YOs—into compliance with the ATA. They were simply too small to compete in the trade, and the anticipated cost of bringing them into compliance was too great.[9] By early 2004, Western Pioneer's operational fleet was down to four vessels, the *Bluefin*, *Redfin*, *Yellowfin*, and *Bowfin*.[a][10] Max Soriano's son Larry, who had risen to become president of Western Pioneer, described the company's cargo business at that time as "working very hard to earn a little money."[11]

With no relief in sight, Western Pioneer abruptly terminated its shipping operations in the spring of 2005. The decision was not widely expected. In fact, three of the company's vessels were at sea when the crews received word that they were on their last voyage.

According to Larry Soriano, the dearth of southbound cargo was the fundamental reason for leaving the trade. Given the amount of cargo available, he felt that there was realistically room for only one carrier. CTI, whose owner, Peter Strong, genuinely enjoyed the business, could have it. The benefit to Western Pioneer of leaving the cargo trade was that it freed up capital and enabled management to focus on other priorities. Soriano characterized the break-bulk transportation business as something of a "dying ember."[12]

a   The *Bowfin*, a former YO, had been granted an extension of its ATA loadline exemption until January 1, 2008.

Coastal Nomad at the Coastal Transportation dock at Dutch Harbor in 2008.

CHAPTER 12

The Business of Coastal Transportation

WITH THE DEMISE OF WESTERN PIONEER'S CARGO OPERATIONS, CTI became the last break-bulk marine shipping operation in the United States. Despite Larry Soriano's claim, the break-bulk marine transportation business is not a dying ember, but a viable specialized niche service. It is an efficient way to provide service to many of the remote ports, floating processors, and catcher/processors in the Aleutian trade area.

CTI is, of course, subject to the same economic forces as Western Pioneer had been. But with its primary competition out of the picture, the company's prospects brightened somewhat. CTI bought Western Pioneer's four operational vessels. It quickly sold the *Bluefin* and *Bowfin*, and kept what it considered to be the two most capable ships, the *Redfin* and *Yellowfin*. These were renamed, respectively, *Coastal Nomad* and *Coastal Progress*. The company had no intention of utilizing them beyond the Aleutian trade area and, to reduce operating costs, allowed their Coast Guard Certificates of Inspection to lapse.

Why would a seafood processor transport frozen cargo in a small ship when containers—what one historian called "the basic building block of the world's transportation system"—are so readily available?[1] In the very competitive transportation industry, one would be inclined to consider *price* as the most important factor. A more comprehensive answer is actually *value*, of which price is only one component. In the Aleutian trade (as well as in many other industries), the value provided by small freighters consists basically of three elements:

Flexibility and Versatility. The aphorism "time is money" is especially applicable to commercial fishermen; time spent in port is time spent not fishing. CTI is capable of serving large or small ports or floating processors on schedules that offer both convenience and efficiency. The service provided by container ships, in contrast, is structured around rigid schedules to established terminals.

CTI's small freighters can easily accommodate both large and small shipments. As well, odd-sized items can be carried on deck.

In Dutch Harbor, there is also the "Quickie Mart factor." CTI's cargo terminal at Dutch Harbor, which consists of 900 feet of dock, sorting areas, and approximately 45 refrigerated vans for interim storage, never really closes and can easily accommodate even the smallest shipments. A vessel can maximize its own schedule by loading or discharging cargo at whatever time it determines to be most efficient.

Speed. Though slower than container ships, the small freighters are faster than tugboats pulling barges loaded with containers. Again, time is money.

Cargo Environment. The holds of ships provide a safer and more stable environment than containers. This is due to three factors:

a. Containers, each with a self-contained refrigeration unit, are checked when loaded aboard a ship or barge, and sometimes ignored until the vessel reaches its destination. "Heavy weather" might prevent repairs to a mechanical malfunction. In contrast, the holds on a freighter are continuously monitored by personnel who can take corrective action if a problem arises.

b. In containers, frigid air is circulated to keep the product frozen. This can cause dehydration of the product. CTI's freighters, in contrast, utilize coil refrigeration in which no air is circulated.

c. The thermal mass and the higher mass-to-surface-area ratio provided by a cargo hold full of frozen product add a significant measure of stability to the hold's environment. Because of the ratio between the volume

The dock at Chignik, Alaska, in 1939. Compare to the photo on the right.

of the cargo and the surface area that surrounds it, traditional holds are also more thermally efficient than shipment in containers. Cold is "lost" through the surface area. The greater the amount of surface area in relation to the volume of cargo, the more cold that is lost.

As an example, in 2011 the lower forward hold of the *Coastal Nomad*—then roughly typical of CTI's fleet—had a capacity of about 17,200 cubic feet and an internal surface area of about 5,200 square feet. The capacity-to-surface-area ratio for this hold was approximately 3.3:1 (3.3 cubic feet of volume to each square foot of surface area). A standard 40-foot container, in contrast, has a capacity of about 1,985 cubic feet and an internal surface area of about 1,224 square feet. The capacity-to-surface-area ratio of the container is approximately

1.6:1, about half that of the *Coastal Nomad*'s hold. The higher capacity-to-surface-area ratio also contributes to the stability of the hold's temperature. Furthermore, both efficiency and stability are increased significantly when the upper forward hold is also in operation because the two holds share a common surface area. (The upper hold's deck is the lower hold's overhead.)

Another factor that favors holds over containers is the amount of insulation. Refrigerated cargo holds are usually insulated with about six inches of blown-in urethane foam insulation. Containers, on the other hand, have a little less than three inches.

In addition to the aforementioned value factors, the economics of operating small scheduled break-bulk freighters compares favorably with that of other forms of

Coastal Navigator approaching the cannery dock in Chignik in 2008, 69 years after the photo at left was taken.

marine transportation available in the Bering Sea area. The small freighters are far more fuel-efficient than tugs pulling barges. One need only look at marine transport in Europe, where fuel prices have been structurally very high for many years. Frozen fish from Northern Europe are transported on small freighters, not by tug and barge. Tramper vessels, because of their size and design, are probably more fuel-efficient than the small freighters, but since the trampers carry cargo only one way, their total fuel costs per cargo ton-mile are higher than for the small freighters. (The tramper service to the Aleutian Islands area is structured around transporting product to Europe and the Far East.) Fully loaded container ships are very efficient overall, but lack the flexibility to provide the type of service offered by small freighters.

To the above four factors one must add reliability. CTI operates six vessels in the Aleutian trade. Round-trip voyages between Seattle and the Aleutian Islands area typically take about 25 days, and this number of vessels allows the company to consistently maintain the weekly scheduled departures that customers rely on and appreciate, while providing ample time for proper maintenance and repair.

With today's modern communications, a vessel departing Seattle will have its position constantly relayed via satellite to Seattle and can be tracked, along with the current sea conditions on the route, by customers at CTI's Internet site (www.coastaltransportation.com). A "wheelhouse report," also available on the Internet site, gives the vessel's estimated times of arrival and departure (ETA and ETD) for the next port to be visited.[2]

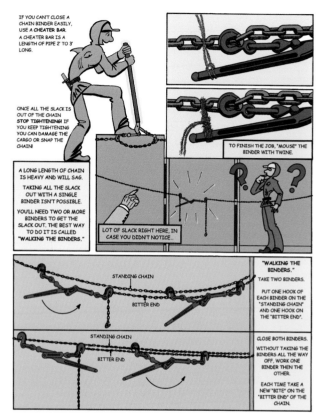

The uniqueness of Coastal Transportation's cargo operations requires it to produce its own training manuals. These are sample pages from *Seamanship for Beginners* and *Life at Sea*.

Operational Hazards

CTI's history, like those of its predecessors and contemporaries, has most assuredly not been one of perpetually calm seas and fair winds. Weather-related incidents aside, there have been problems: some quite serious and many easily avoidable. For example, in September 1996, the throttle on the company's *Mokuhana* (later renamed *Coastal Pilot*) failed in the Lake Washington Ship Canal because a valve had inadvertently been left closed after a routine maintenance procedure. The out-of-control ship smashed into a dock and four vessels as a result. Fortunately, no one was injured. In October of the following year, the *Coastal Trader* caught fire in the Gulf of Alaska while en route to Seattle. The crew safely evacuated and was rescued by the Coast Guard. Though its frozen cargo was salvaged, the vessel was a total loss. The cause of the fire, which began in the engine room, was never determined.[3] And then there was the time in 1989 that Seattle's evening news featured images of the *Mokuhana* aground on Whidbey Island, in Puget Sound. The vessel's captain had been drinking while cargo was being offloaded at Bellingham, and had fallen asleep at the helm.

Incidents such as these are among the perils associated with the maritime transport business. The company's vessels, though hardly new, are well maintained and functionally up-to-date. Beginning in 1995, the company's standards for its mariners became more rigorous, mirroring a change in the maritime industry as a whole. The company initiated a program in which captains and crews were and continue to be vetted, tested, and monitored. To facilitate safe and efficient vessel operations, Port Captain George Collazo has produced a comprehensive vessel operations manual that is specifically tailored to CTI's operations. The manual draws considerably from the experiences of CTI captains and deckhands. It was written, in Collazo's words, "by mariners for mariners, and in a way mariners can understand." The publication lists the company's standing orders, policies, and standard procedures, and addresses almost every imaginable contingency at sea. Notably, it contains stark accounts of mistakes that were made, and discusses how similar mishaps can be avoided in the future. Collazo has also written (and illustrated) CTI's comic-book-format manual *Seamanship for Beginners* (2008), which is geared toward new employees and covers subjects such as vessel nomenclature, knot tying, securing cargo, and, of course, safety.

The end of the 1990s saw a number of deadly mishaps throughout the Alaskan fishing industry, forcing it into a major swing toward safety training. Nor was the U.S. fishing industry alone. Safety had become a major concern for mariners everywhere. The result was an international treaty implementing what came to be called the Standards of Training, Certification and Watchkeeping (STCW). Enforced by the Coast Guard in the United States, these regulations mandated, among other things, increased safety training.

Stung by its own close calls, Coastal Transportation became one of only two ship operators in the United States that have their own Coast Guard–approved firefighting simulator. With nearly 4,000 interior square feet and a height of three decks, the structure also enables training for medical emergencies and more common contingencies such as Freon gas leaks.

But one indisputable fact remains: accidents, most of them avoidable, will happen. Captains and crews can have the best intentions and the best equipment and training available, but no one can mandate good judgment, and even the best equipment will periodically fail. (As this is being written, the *Queen Elizabeth II*, Britain's flagship passenger liner, is aground on a well-known sandbar on the southern English coast.[4])

And then there is the eternal challenge of being at sea in relatively small vessels, in Alaska, during the winter. The following are two contemporary examples of CTI vessels and crews operating under extreme conditions.

COASTAL PROGRESS, MARCH 2007

March can be a brutal month on Alaska's marine waters. Winter conditions still prevail, and storms can be severe in this season of change. One of the worst March storms in CTI's experience occurred in 2007.

The *Coastal Progress*, under Captain Taylor Campbell, a veteran Alaska hand, was a day out of Sand Point, the voyage's first port-of-call on its northbound leg. With a cargo load of 650,000 pounds, the vessel was carrying only a quarter of its capacity. For the sake of stability, Campbell would have preferred a full load of cargo. After days of continuous rolling in the Gulf of Alaska, the crew looked forward to getting into more protected waters.

Campbell finished his watch at noon and retired to his stateroom. Not long afterward, his vessel began taking some very hard rolls. Concerned about the possibility of cargo shifting and being damaged, Campbell hurried to the pilothouse. In the short while he had been off watch, the wind had increased dramatically and the seas had grown precipitously. As well, the temperature had dropped. A large high-pressure system in the Bering Sea region and a low-pressure system in the Gulf of Alaska had conspired to send frigid air streaming across the Alaska Peninsula. Directly affecting the *Coastal Progress* was a strong, bitterly cold wind that was blowing far out to sea from Wide Bay, which was to the north-northwest of the vessel. The wind continued to increase, the seas continued to build, and, perhaps most ominously, the temperature was plummeting.

Campbell had to make a decision: retreat back into the Gulf of Alaska or forge ahead. He chose the latter for two reasons: he had a lot of confidence in his vessel, and to retreat would put them into even larger seas and could set their schedule back a week or more. It helped psychologically that he could see land (Chirikof Island) on the radar. Ice began building on the *Coastal Progress*'s superstructure, but there was little the crew could do to remove it. The wind was blowing a steady 75 knots, and gusting to 90. The seas were up to 35 feet high, made sharper and steeper by the area's tidal currents. And they were on their own; in these conditions, a Coast Guard helicopter, even if it deployed, would be unable to assist them.

There was the real danger that a large wave would break out one or more pilothouse windows and damage critical navigation, communication, and vessel control equipment. So to minimize the risk, Campbell steered and throttled the vessel by hand, slowing down and facing directly into the largest waves, then throttling up and resuming his course when the wave had passed. The temperature dropped to 4 degrees Fahrenheit, and ice continued to build. The antennas for the VHF radio and satellite telephone snapped off. Fortunately, the critically important radars were mounted above where the ice was building and continued to function. The forward pilothouse windows were covered with a thick layer of ice, and there was a lot of concern for the steel visor above them. Ice had accumulated so heavily that the visor was beginning to flex. The visor eventually received structural support when its ice grew together with ice that had built up from the rail below.

After a long and harrowing night, the *Coastal Progress* made it to the Semidi Islands early the next morning. The islands offered some protection, but not enough to anchor. Campbell put a crew on deck to begin chipping at the ice, which was rock-hard, blue-tinted, and in some places several feet thick. Heavy sea smoke covered the water. The crew made a little progress on the ice before the vessel departed for Sand Point, which was 12 hours away under good traveling conditions.

The *Coastal Progress* continued to add ice most of the way to Sand Point, but she arrived safely at three o'clock the following morning. A strong, bitterly cold wind was blowing from the north, and the channel buoys in the harbor were

Peter and Leslie Strong met on Cordova, Alaska's waterfront in 1976. They worked together tendering salmon in Alaska before starting Coastal Transportation in 1984.

capsized from the weight of accumulated ice. A tug and barge moored to the city dock were pinned there and completely coated in ice. Everything on the deck of the *Coastal Progress* was completely frozen together, and it took fully 12 hours for the crew just to prepare the vessel for docking. Once it was safely moored, the massive job of removing the ice began. Someone lent them a chain saw, which was used to cut away the ice that covered the pilothouse's front windows and other areas. One estimate was that the *Coastal Progress* had accumulated 150 to 200 tons of ice.

The *Coastal Progress* spent two weeks discharging and loading cargo in the Aleutian Islands area, and it was still carrying a substantial amount of ice when it finally departed, fully loaded, for Seattle. The last of the ice did not melt away until the vessel was three days out of Seattle.

Taylor Campbell called this storm a 25-year event. In 1982, he had endured similar storm conditions in the Gulf of Alaska that he considered to have been even more perilous because he was on Western Pioneer's *Dolphin*, a smaller and less-capable vessel, and they were days away from land (see footnote on page 79).[5]

COASTAL NOMAD, JANUARY 2008

Arthur Lynch, also a veteran of the trade, was in command of the *Coastal Nomad* in January 2008. He was at St. Paul, in the Pribilof Islands, where he was scheduled to rendezvous with two catcher/processor vessels to transfer cargoes of frozen cod. The plan was to anchor just inside the harbor and have a vessel tie to each side of the *Coastal Nomad* so that their cargoes could be transferred simultaneously. The Bering Sea's southern ice edge was not too far to the north, and it was snowing and very cold. The forecast called for 50-knot winds from the north. These conditions, though harsh, were not out of the ordinary for this time of year.

The first vessel was delayed, but the 124-foot *Bering*

Leader was there and ready. A large swell was running from the south-southwest and surging into the harbor, and as the *Bering Leader* maneuvered to get alongside the *Coastal Nomad*, a surge caught it and the vessel smashed hard against the freighter. Their original plan was not going to work in these conditions, and Lynch quickly decided to moor to a dock in the inner harbor and have the *Bering Leader* tie to his outside. His crew secured the *Coastal Nomad* to the dock with more than a dozen lines before the *Bering Leader* came alongside. Crab buoy-like fenders, some six feet tall, served as cushions between the two vessels' steel hulls. After nearly 24 hours of essentially nonstop work, the cargo transfer was completed and the *Bering Leader* untied. It was immediately replaced by another catcher/processor, the *Alaska Leader*. A second catcher/processor, the *Bering Prowler*, tied to the harbor's fuel dock and the crew began bringing product by forklift.

Unfortunately, the weather began to deteriorate rapidly and to a degree far beyond what the forecasters had expected. The wind blew from the northeast at a steady 75 knots and gusted to 100 knots, hitting the two vessels bow-on. At the same time, the surge washing into the harbor was lifting the vessels' sterns and forcing them ahead.

The surge repeatedly pushed the *Alaska Leader* against the *Coastal Nomad* so hard that the fenders began popping. To little avail, the crews lowered wood pallets and bundles of life jackets between the boats. More alarmingly, the lines that secured the *Coastal Nomad* to the dock began parting. There was the very real danger that the additional strain on the remaining lines would cause them to part, and the *Coastal Nomad* and *Alaska Leader* would be adrift in the harbor with little room to maneuver. If this happened, both vessels would likely be smashed against the breakwater. To take some of the strain off the mooring lines, Lynch gingerly powered his vessel ahead with the main engine to counter the wind and used his bow thruster to keep his vessel pinned to the dock. But because of the combination of the wind, the surge, and Lynch's maneuvering, the *Alaska Leader* would sometimes "slingshot" past the *Coastal Nomad*, and it, too, began parting lines. Lynch put some of his crew aboard the *Alaska Leader* to assist with tending lines. He also had the crew keep fire axes handy in case it was necessary to quickly sever the *Coastal Nomad*'s ties to the dock and/or the *Alaska Leader*.

Despite the brutal conditions, the *Coastal Nomad*'s crew simultaneously loaded cargo on both the port and starboard sides. By the time the last of the cargo was transferred, the crew, except for a few breaks, had worked nearly 48 hours straight.[a] But now they could mostly relax while their vessel, fully laden, departed St. Paul and made its way to Seattle. Arthur Lynch characterized the whole ordeal—working extremely long hours through hurricane-force winds in subfreezing temperatures—as "not routine, but what we expect, and what we do."[6]

• • •

INFRASTRUCTURE AT DUTCH HARBOR

There is an air of makeshift utilitarianism in Dutch Harbor that is embodied in its use of shipping containers. The rugged units are used conventionally as independent storage units for supplies and equipment. They are, as well, converted into shops, offices, and even living spaces. Mostly, however, they are used to store frozen fish. At any given time, approximately 1,000 are so employed. Each uses a considerable amount of energy, and in total they constitute a major drain on the local electric utility. For storing large volumes of product, this system is also thermally inefficient because of the containers' high surface-area-to-volume ratio and fairly minimal insulation.

In 2009, the Alaska seafood-processing titan American Seafoods formed a subsidiary, DH Ports, to join with the European cold-storage company Kloosterboer in the construction of a $150 million multi-use cargo terminal that includes a 30,000-ton-capacity cold storage and a 900-foot dock. To help minimize damage to frozen cargo, the facility features an enclosed sorting atrium into which processing boats can offload product to avoid damage to packaging and product due to exposure to the elements, long a problem in Dutch Harbor.

---

a Ironically, one of the most comfortable jobs was working in the refrigerated holds: Though the temperature was below zero, there was no wind and it wasn't snowing.

THE FUTURE OF POLLOCK

About the same time that Western Pioneer left the transportation business, there was a significant development in the pollock fishery of the Bering Sea/Aleutian Islands area. The fishery was certified as sustainable by the London-based Marine Stewardship Council, an independent, global, nonprofit organization that is working to reverse the decline of the world's fisheries.[7] Certification was sought by the At-Sea Processors Association, a fisheries trade group, at the urging of European seafood buyers. Europeans in particular have shown a preference for "eco-labeled" products.

Certification was awarded in 2004. Several months later, Unilever, one of the world's largest buyers of fish, announced the availability in Germany of "fish fingers made from sustainable Alaskan pollock." In addition to providing a significant marketing advantage, the independent assessment of policies and practices used in managing and conducting the fishery provided the industry with valuable insights into its own operations and helps to foster efficiency and—important also to associated businesses—long-term stability.[8]

The certification of the pollock fishery as sustainable, however, is no guarantee of stability. In 2006, biologists estimated that the biomass of pollock in the Bering Sea was the lowest it had been in more than a decade. During the 2007 fishing season, U.S. fishermen fell 40,000 metric tons (88 million pounds) short of their 1,394,000 metric ton quota. Some fishermen, who had been accustomed to fishing within 60 miles of Dutch Harbor, were traveling 500 miles in search of fish. A few years later, the biomass was back up, leaving scientists to argue whether natural fluctuation was the culprit or, on the other hand, if a major population crash was in the works.

The National Marine Fisheries Service, which has jurisdiction over the eastern Bering Sea pollock resource, has set the 2012 quota at 1,200,000 metric tons, about 4 percent lower than the 1,252,000 metric ton limit in 2011. The average catch of pollock in the eastern Bering Sea for the years 1977 through 2011 was 1,168,097 metric tons.[9]

Coastal Navigator (beneath the sun) anchored near the mouth of the Naknek River in Bristol Bay.

The Future of the Aleutian Trade

The Aleutian trade as we know it today began developing shortly after World War II to serve the fledgling Bering Sea king crab industry. It peaked in about 1990, when some 20 small freighters carried cargo for hire between Puget Sound and the Aleutian Islands area. By 2005, that number had been reduced to six, though the average size of these vessels is considerably larger than that of their predecessors. All of the vessels currently in the trade are owned by CTI, the last break-bulk marine cargo carrier in the United States.

Seattle today is widely recognized as a modern, progressive city that has spawned innovative computer software companies such as Microsoft and trend-setting firms like Starbucks. CTI, which is also headquartered there, is more a part of the traditional working-class economy that built the city. Maritime transport has long contributed to the diversity and vibrancy of Seattle's economy and culture. Except for the fact that it does not transport passengers, CTI is in a limited respect a microcosm of the once-proud Alaska Steamship Co., the carrier that tied Seattle to Alaska. Seattle's maritime activities—at least in the downtown area—are no longer as apparent as they once were, but they remain an integral and important element of the city's diverse economy and culture.

In 1909, *The American Review of Reviews* wrote that industrial and commercial Alaska was "to all intents and purposes, annexed to Seattle."[1] In a broad context, that statement is hardly true today, because large multinational corporations have a commanding presence in the 49th state. It is true, however, that the fishing industry in the Bering Sea today is far more closely associated with Seattle than Alaska. Efficiency demands streamlined transportation between producers and markets and that there is no unnecessary redundancy.

Dutch Harbor is today an industrial outpost of Seattle of the first magnitude. But the industry has benefited from being part of Alaska because of the state and federal governments' largesse in developing infrastructure. Some of the money used to construct the harbors at St. Paul and St. George and similar facilities was provided by the flush-with-oil-revenues State of Alaska. Most, though, was federal money, adeptly secured by the late Alaska Senator Ted Stevens.

As well as being the last break-bulk maritime shipping operation in the United States, CTI is the last direct beneficiary of the Aleutian Trade Act of 1990. Its fleet of six vessels are among those grandfathered into the trade and operate under the regulatory exemptions provided by the legislation. Economic stability has never been a hallmark of the Aleutian Islands region. Like the sudden williwaws that define the region's weather, prosperity comes and goes. Consider the wealth generated by sea otter pelts, seal skins, salt cod, crabs, and, most recently, products based on the region's vast groundfish resource.

The Economist magazine characterized commercial fishermen as the "last race of hunter-gatherers."[2] The fishing industry is a gamble: fish stocks can fluctuate dramatically, markets can be fickle, and the regulations that govern fisheries can be modified for a host of reasons. The crab boom of the 1970s and 1980s drew fishermen and fish processors to the Bering Sea in droves. Fishing companies proliferated. Some prospered, some went bust, while others merged or were sold off. Small fortunes were made and lost in the process.

Dutch Harbor is today the nation's largest fishing port (by volume), and there is a solid niche for a small ocean freight company that is able to serve the specialized needs of the port and the surrounding region. But any company participating in the Aleutian cargo trade over the long term must be prepared to weather changes. A combination of versatility, efficiency, reliability, and close attention to customers' needs has been key to Coastal Transportation's success.

During the early 1990s, a typical Aleutian freighter had a cargo-carrying capacity of less than 40,000 cubic feet. Today, a vessel of such limited capacity could not be operated profitably. As well, high fuel consumption has been an ongoing concern. The fuel problem was especially acute with the two former Western Pioneer ships *Coastal Progress* and *Coastal Nomad*. The sister ships had been constructed in the 1980s as oil platform supply vessels, and little consideration had been given to fuel economy. Each vessel consumed more than 3,000 gallons per day—about twice the Aleutian trade norm.

A basic rule of naval architecture is that for a vessel of a given width, the longer the vessel's waterline length, the less power that is required to achieve a given speed. A naval architect's analysis of the *Coastal Progress* and *Coastal Nomad* in 2006 recommended adding a stern extension with a sleeker hydrodynamic form and a bulbous bow to each vessel. At that time, fuel prices were rising to all-time highs, and CTI decided to follow the architect's advice. As well, the company decided to install new main engines on each vessel. The upgrades were accomplished in 2006 and 2007, and the result was very satisfactory: fuel consumption dropped by nearly half.

CTI's next major project was to increase the size of the *Coastal Navigator*'s cargo holds by cutting her in half and adding a midsection. But the new section could not be added just anywhere. When possible, captains of Aleutian freighters prefer to dock their ships where both the forward and aft cargo holds can be worked simultaneously. The docks at the ports used by CTI vessels vary considerably, and to determine the optimal distances between the lengthened vessel's hatches and the geometry of her cargo gear, Tim Shaffer, CTI's general manager, and John Fisker-Andersen, the company's port engineer—tape measures in hand—traveled to King Cove and Dutch Harbor. There they carefully measured the docks regularly used by CTI vessels. As well, they queried boat captains and seafood plant managers.

As a result of this homework, in 2010 a new section was added aft of the *Coastal Navigator*'s aft hatch, and a stern extension and a bulbous bow were added as well. The vessel's length grew from 195 to 261 feet. The result was an increase in her cargo capacity from 60,000 to 98,280 cubic feet, with no increase in fuel consumption. As well, the vessel's appearance became remarkably elegant. At the same time as her lengthening, the *Coastal Navigator*'s refrigeration system was updated to keep pace with ever-tightening requirements for the carriage of frozen seafood, and state-of-the-art LED lighting fixtures were added to the cargo holds.

In 2011, the 214-foot *Coastal Progress* was lengthened to 260 feet, an improvement that increased her cargo capacity from 72,000 to 100,000 cubic feet. A third set of cargo gear was also added. A similar lengthening and improving of the *Coastal Nomad* is ongoing.

Fortunately, there is no sunset provision contained in the Aleutian Trade Act, so it is possible to construct a new ship for the trade. Federal law requires that vessels carrying freight between U.S. ports be constructed in domestic shipyards, which tend to be more expensive than their foreign counterparts (particularly those in the Far East) but have high standards of workmanship.

Peter Strong, CTI's president, believes it is feasible—particularly during lean economic times, when shipyards are hungry for business—to construct a new ship for the Aleutian trade. He has a design in mind that is based on vessels currently in use in Europe. As conceived today, a "third generation" Aleutian trade vessel would be designed primarily to efficiently handle cargo palletized for transport in containers. Most cargo carried north by CTI comes out of containers, and most cargo carried south goes into containers. The cargo is normally palletized in dimensions that maximize the use of the space in a container. The hypothetical vessel's upper and lower holds would each have a depth about equal to the inside height of a standard container. Palletized cargo would not be lowered into the hold through a traditional hatch in a deck, but forklifted into the upper holds through side ports—basically large waterproof doors in the vessel's hull. Elevators would provide access to the lower holds. Strong estimates that the cost of a vessel with a capacity of 100,000 cubic feet would be about 20 to 25 million dollars.

The technology and materials incorporated into a third-generation Aleutian trade vessel would be, of course, a vast improvement over those that were available when vessels such as the *Starr* and *Western Pioneer* were built and operated. Western Alaska's waters, however, have not changed. They remain as formidable as ever and will continue to be a challenge to both vessels and crews.

Name } *DORA*
Former Name } *DORA*
Official Number } **N/A**
Registered Dimensions (feet) Length x Beam x Draft } **112 x 27 x 13**
Built/Converted (Modified to ATA) } **1880**
Disposition } **Wrecked, 1920**

Name } *FERN*
Former Name } *USLHS Fern*
Official Number } **234815**
Registered Dimensions (feet) Length x Beam x Draft } **103 x 22 x 9.5**
Built/Converted (Modified to ATA) } **1915**
Disposition } **Scrapped**

Name } *GARLAND*
Former Name } *FS-248 US Army*
Official Number } **250431**
Registered Dimensions (feet) Length x Beam x Draft } **139 x 33 x 16**
Built/Converted (Modified to ATA) } **1944**
Disposition } **N/A**

Name } *EXPANSION*
Former Name } *FS-37 US Army*
Official Number } **254797**
Registered Dimensions (feet) Length x Beam x Draft } **107 x 27 x 12**
Built/Converted (Modified to ATA) } **1942**
Disposition } **Sold, renamed *Temehani*, sank at Bora Bora in 1982**

Name } *SCULPIN*
Former Name } *YOG-35 USN*
Official Number } **587573**
Registered Dimensions (feet) Length x Beam x Draft } **166 x 32 x 15**
Built/Converted (Modified to ATA) } **1943/1978**
Disposition } **Sold, foreign**

Name } *TARPON*
Former Name } *YO-201 USN*
Official Number } **576033**
Registered Dimensions (feet) Length x Beam x Draft } **166 x 32 x 15**
Built/Converted (Modified to ATA) } **1944/1976**
Disposition } **Sold, foreign**

Name } *DOLPHIN (2)*
Former Name } *YO-248 USN*
Official Number } **617019**
Registered Dimensions (feet) Length x Beam x Draft } **166 x 32 x 15**
Built/Converted (Modified to ATA) } **1944/1980**
Disposition } **Sold, foreign**

Name } *WESTERN PIONEER*
Former Name } *ARS-29, USNF Vent*
Official Number } **277305**
Registered Dimensions (feet) Length x Beam x Draft } **173 x 37 x 19**
Built/Converted (Modified to ATA) } **1944/1958**
Disposition } **Total loss (fire), 1975**

Name } *SNOWBIRD*
Former Name } *FSR-399 US Army*
Official Number } **501812**
Registered Dimensions (feet) Length x Beam x Draft } **166 x 32 x 12**
Built/Converted (Modified to ATA) } **1944/1972**
Disposition } **Converted to catcher vessel, now *Ballyhoo***

Name } *STARR*
Former Name } *STARR*
Official Number } **210542**
Registered Dimensions (feet) Length x Beam x Draft } **131 x 26 x 20**
Built/Converted (Modified to ATA) } **1912**
Disposition } **Scrapped, 1940**

Name } *WESTERN TRADER*
Former Name } *KAILUA*
Official Number } **220754**
Registered Dimensions (feet) Length x Beam x Draft } **120 x 24 x 10**
Built/Converted (Modified to ATA) } **1920**
Disposition } **Sold, foreign, 1960**

Name } *ALEUT PACKER*
Former Name } *YO-168 USN*
Official Number } **580852**
Registered Dimensions (feet) Length x Beam x Draft } **156 x 31 x 13**
Built/Converted (Modified to ATA) } **1943/1985**
Disposition } **Converted to longliner, now *Blue Gadus***

Name } *MARLIN*
Former Name } *YO-169 USN*
Official Number } **568721**
Registered Dimensions (feet) Length x Beam x Draft } **156 x 31 x 13**
Built/Converted (Modified to ATA) } **1944/1975**
Disposition } **Sold, foreign**

Name } *BOWFIN*
Former Name } *YO-133 USN*
Official Number } **604231**
Registered Dimensions (feet) Length x Beam x Draft } **166 x 32 x 15**
Built/Converted (Modified to ATA) } **1944/1979**
Disposition } **Sold, foreign**

Name } *CAPELIN*
Former Name } *YO-76 USN*
Official Number } **506241**
Registered Dimensions (feet) Length x Beam x Draft } **166 x 32 x 15**
Built/Converted (Modified to ATA) } **1944/1988**
Disposition } **Laid up, Seattle, 2012**

Name } *POLAR PIONEER*
Former Name } *Lucidor AF-45*
Official Number } **250135**
Registered Dimensions (feet) Length x Beam x Draft } **323 x 50 x 26**
Built/Converted (Modified to ATA) } **1945/1967**
Disposition } **Sold, foreign**

Name } *COASTAL VOYAGER*
Former Name } *Cpl John J Plinder Jr, Viceroy*
Official Number } **284906**
Registered Dimensions (feet) Length x Beam x Draft } **166 x 32 x 12**
Built/Converted (Modified to ATA) } **1945/1986**
Disposition } **Converted to catcher, now** *Western Queen*

Name } *DENALI*
Former Name } *F.E. Lovejoy*
Official Number } **250021**
Registered Dimensions (feet) Length x Beam x Draft } **170 x 36 x 12**
Built/Converted (Modified to ATA) } **1946/1975**
Disposition } **Converted to fish processor** *Pacific Producer*

Name } *PRIBILOF*
Former Name } *FSR-791 US Army*
Official Number } **293151**
Registered Dimensions (feet) Length x Beam x Draft } **204 x 38 x 17**
Built/Converted (Modified to ATA) } **1954/1975**
Disposition } **Converted to fish processing vessel**

Name } *COASTAL SEA*
Former Name } *Sunmar Sea*
Official Number } **666754**
Registered Dimensions (feet) Length x Beam x Draft } **176 x 34 x 12**
Built/Converted (Modified to ATA) } **1956/1984**
Disposition } **In service, CTI**

Name } *COASTAL NOMAD* (1)
Former Name } *Blue Peter II, Biscayne Freeze*
Official Number } **686157**
Registered Dimensions (feet) Length x Beam x Draft } **208 x 35 x 12**
Built/Converted (Modified to ATA) } **1964/1985**
Disposition } **Sold, foreign, 2003**

Name } *COASTAL NOMAD* (2)
Former Name } *Redfin*
Official Number } **656674**
Registered Dimensions (feet) Length x Beam x Draft } **256 x 40 x 20**
Built/Converted (Modified to ATA) } **1986**
Disposition } **In service, CTI, lengthened, 2012**

Name } *EASTERN WIND*
Former Name } *n/a*
Official Number } **964583**
Registered Dimensions (feet) Length x Beam x Draft } **220 x 41 x 18**
Built/Converted (Modified to ATA) } **1990**
Disposition } **In service, Trident Seafoods**

Name } *COASTAL TRADER* (1)
Former Name } *FS-232 US Army, Theresa Lee*
Official Number } **285716**
Registered Dimensions (feet) Length x Beam x Draft } **168 x 32 x 12**
Built/Converted (Modified to ATA) } **1945/1984**
Disposition } **Scrapped, 1998**

Name } *COASTAL RANGER*
Former Name } *YW-102 USN, Double Star*
Official Number } **520075**
Registered Dimensions (feet) Length x Beam x Draft } **166 x 32 x 15**
Built/Converted (Modified to ATA) } **1945/1989**
Disposition } **Laid up, Seattle, 2012**

Name } *COASTAL PILOT*
Former Name } *Mokuhana*
Official Number } **266658**
Registered Dimensions (feet) Length x Beam x Draft } **166 x 36 x 11**
Built/Converted (Modified to ATA) } **1953**
Disposition } **Sold, now** *Integrity*

Name } *DOLPHIN* (1)
Former Name } *New Tide*
Official Number } **270744**
Registered Dimensions (feet) Length x Beam x Draft } **117 x 31 x 8**
Built/Converted (Modified to ATA) } **1955/1972**
Disposition } **Sold, foreign**

Name } *COASTAL TRADER* (2)
Former Name } *Sunmar Sky*
Official Number } **683227**
Registered Dimensions (feet) Length x Beam x Draft } **243 x 44 x 15**
Built/Converted (Modified to ATA) } **1963/1985**
Disposition } **In service, CTI**

Name } *COASTAL MERCHANT*
Former Name } *Berthe Dancoast*
Official Number } **1038382**
Registered Dimensions (feet) Length x Beam x Draft } **209 x 34 x 15**
Built/Converted (Modified to ATA) } **1966/1995**
Disposition } **In service, CTI**

Name } *COASTAL PROGRESS*
Former Name } *Yellowfin*
Official Number } **927811**
Registered Dimensions (feet) Length x Beam x Draft } **256 x 40 x 20**
Built/Converted (Modified to ATA) } **1988**
Disposition } **In service, CTI, lengthened, 2011**

Name } *COASTAL NAVIGATOR*
Former Name } *Northern Wind*
Official Number } **969815**
Registered Dimensions (feet) Length x Beam x Draft } **261 x 41 x 18**
Built/Converted (Modified to ATA) } **1991**
Disposition } **In service, CTI, lengthened, 2010**

Fleet List compiled by Peter Strong

ENDNOTES

ENDNOTES

INTRODUCTION

1 Adm. F. A. Zeusler, USCG (Ret.), "'Cooperation': The Key to Alaska's Shipping Problem," *Alaska Life* (September 1947): 10.
2 D. E. Skinner, "The Alaskan Trade," Proceedings of the American Merchant Marine Conference, 1962, p. 28.
3 John Gray, "Alaska's Unique Transportation System," *Alaska Review of Social and Economic Conditions* (June 1980): 1.
4 Coastal Transportation, Inc., *Vessel Operation Manual*, 3rd ed., December 2006, 6-3.
5 Photo explanation, *Aleutian Eagle*, January 6, 1989.
6 *U.S. Coast Pilot 9, Pacific and Arctic Coasts Alaska: Cape Spencer to Beaufort Sea*, 25th ed. (Washington, DC: National Ocean Service, 2007), 432, http://www.nauticalcharts.noaa.gov/nsd/coastpilot9.htm (accessed June 8, 2009).
7 George Collazo, port captain, Coastal Transportation, Inc., personal communication with author, June 16, 2009.
8 *U.S. Coast Pilot, Alaska, Part II: Yakutat Bay to Arctic Ocean*, 4th ed. (Washington, DC: GPO, 1938), 3; U.S. Army Corps of Engineers, *The Ports of Alaska* (Washington, DC: GPO, 1984), 78.
9 Photo caption, *Aleutian Eagle*, January 6, 1989.
10 Taylor Campbell, captain, Coastal Transportation, Inc., personal communication with author, January 19, 2009; *U.S. Coast Pilot, Alaska, Aleutian Islands*, 1st ed. (Washington, DC: GPO, 1944), 1.
11 *U.S. Coast Pilot 9, Pacific and Arctic Coasts Alaska: Cape Spencer to Beaufort Sea*, 25th ed. (Washington, DC: National Ocean Service, 2007), 433, http://www.nauticalcharts.noaa.gov/nsd/coastpilot9.htm (accessed June 8, 2009).
12 Committee on the Bering Sea Ecosystem, National Research Council, *The Bering Sea Ecosystem* (Washington, DC: National Academies Press, 1996), exec. summary.
13 Grant F. Winthrop, "U.S. Fishermen Gear Up for a Haul Off Alaska," *Fortune* (January 29, 1979): 52.
14 NOAA news release, July 17, 2008, "Dutch Harbor-Unalaska, Alaska, and New Bedford, Mass. Remain Top Fishing Ports," http://www.noaanews.noaa.gov/stories2008/20080717_fishingports.html (accessed June 10, 2009).
15 Marine Stewardship Council, "Alaska Pollock – Bering Sea and Aleutian Islands," December 4, 2007.
16 Wesley Loy, "Catch Limit for Bering Pollock Set to Dive," *Anchorage Daily News*, November 14, 2008.

CHAPTER 1

1 "Sea Otter Hunting," *Alaska Journal* (Autumn 1971): 46 (reprinted from the original *Alaska Journal*, Juneau, May 6, 1893).
2 Thomas A. Bailey, "Why the United States Purchased Alaska," *Pacific Historical Review* (March 1934): 39-49.
3 Ivan Petroff, *Report on the Population, Industries, and Resources of Alaska*, 47th Cong., 2d sess., Ho. Misc. Doc. No. 42, Part 8 (Washington, DC: GPO, 1884), 52.
4 *Seal Fisheries of Alaska*, 44th Cong., 1st sess., 1876, Ho. Ex. Doc. No. 83, p. 243.
5 Ivan Petroff, *Report on the Population, Industries, and Resources of Alaska*, 47th Cong., 2d sess., Ho. Misc. Doc. No. 42, Part 8 (Washington, DC: GPO, 1884), 51.
6 Instructions to Captain Howard, in *Russian America*, 40th Cong., 2d sess., 1868, Ho. Ex. Doc. No. 177, Pt. I, 191; "Report of Assistant George Davidson relative to the coast, features, and resources of Alaska territory," reprinted in *Russian America*, 40th Cong., 2d sess., 1868, Ho. Ex. Doc. No. 177, Pt. I, 254-256.
7 Act of July 27, 1868 (15 Stat. 240).
8 L. A. Lagrange, "Report of L. A. Lagrange, on Unalaska," in *Report of the Secretary of the Interior*, 1869 (Washington, DC: GPO, 1869), 1043.
9 Act to Facilitate the Procurement of Statistics of Trade Between the United States and Its Noncontiguous Territory (32 Stat. 172).
10 "No More Export Declarations on Alaskan and Hawaiian Shipments," *Pacific Marine Review* (May 1948): 76; Foster L. McGovern, "Alaska Duties Total $75,000," *Alaska Life* (June 1940): 18.
11 George S. Boutwell, Secretary of the Treasury, February 9, 1870, in *Fur Seal Fisheries of Alaska*, 41st Cong., 2d sess., February 11, 1870, Ho. Ex. Doc. No. 129.
12 *Seal Fisheries of Alaska*, 44th Cong., 1st sess., Ho. Ex. Doc. No. 83, 1876, p. 194; Herbert E. Yates, "The Decline and Rise of the Fur Seal," *National Fisherman* (April 30, 1978): 102.
13 William H. Dall, *Alaska and Its Resources* (Boston: Lee and Shepard, 1870), 495.
14 Act of July 27, 1868, §6 (15 Stat. 240).
15 George S. Boutwell, Secretary of the Treasury, February 9, 1870, in *Fur Seal Fisheries of Alaska*, 41st Cong., 2d sess., February 11, 1870, Ho. Ex. Doc. No. 129.
16 Henry W. Elliott, *Report on the Condition of the Fur-Seal Fisheries of the Pribylov Islands in 1890* (Paris: Chamerot & Renouard, 1893), 250.
17 Act of March 3, 1869 (15 Stat. 348).
18 Report of Joseph Wilson, inspector of customs, October 26, 1869, in "Reports on Condition of Seal Life on the Pribilof Islands by Special Treasury Agents in Charge, and Others, from 1868 to 1895, both inclusive," in *Seal and Salmon Fisheries and General Resources of Alaska*, Vol. 1 (Washington, DC: GPO, 1898).
19 George S. Boutwell, Secretary of the Treasury, February 9, 1870, in *Fur Seal Fisheries of Alaska*, 41st Cong., 2d sess., February 11, 1870, Ho. Ex. Doc. No. 129.
20 Joseph Wilson, inspector of customs, October 26, 1869, in "Reports on Condition of Seal Life on the Pribilof Islands by Special Treasury Agents in Charge, and Others, from 1868 to 1895, both inclusive," in *Seal and Salmon Fisheries and General Resources of Alaska*, Vol. 1 (Washington, DC: GPO, 1898), 10.
21 "The Fur Industry in Alaska," *Alaska Review of Business and Economic Conditions* (November 1966): 1.
22 George S. Boutwell, Secretary of the Treasury, February 9, 1870, in *Fur Seal Fisheries of Alaska*, 41st Cong., 2d sess., February 11, 1870, Ho. Ex. Doc. No. 129.
23 *Seal Fisheries of Alaska*, 44th Cong., 1st sess., Ho. Ex. Doc. No. 83, 1876, p. 190; Frank B. Norris, *Isolated Paradise: An Administrative History of the Katmai and Aniakchak NPS Units, Alaska* (Anchorage: National Park Service, 1996) unpaged, http://www.nps.gov/archive/katm/adhi/adhi1.htm (accessed April 6, 2008); Alaska Commercial Company, *The Unique and Proud History of Alaska Commercial Company*, http://www.alaskacommercial.com/AboutAC/AboutAC.html (accessed April 6, 2008).
24 Act of July 1, 1870: An Act to Prevent the Extermination of Fur-bearing Animals in Alaska (16 Stat. 180).
25 Copy of lease in *Seal Fisheries of Alaska*, 44th Cong., 1st sess., Ho. Ex. Doc. No. 83, 1876, p. 21.
26 *Seal Fisheries of Alaska*, 44th Cong., 1st sess., Ho. Ex. Doc. No. 83, 1876, pp. 195-196.
27 *Seal Fisheries of Alaska*, 44th Cong., 1st sess., Ho. Ex. Doc. No. 83, 1876, pp. 38, 51.
28 Special [Treasury] Agent H. G. Otis, Annual Report for 1880, in *Seal and Salmon Fisheries and General Resources of Alaska*, Vol. 1 (Washington, DC: GPO, 1898), 136; Annual Report of Special [Treasury] Agent Charles J. Goff, 1889, in *Seal and Salmon Fisheries and General Resources of Alaska*, Vol. 1 (Washington, DC: GPO, 1898), 225; Annual Report of Special [Treasury] Agent Charles J. Goff, 1890, in *Seal and Salmon Fisheries and General Resources of Alaska*, Vol. 1 (Washington, DC: GPO, 1898), 230.
29 Ivan Petroff, *Report on the Population, Industries, and Resources of Alaska* in 47th Cong., 2d sess., Ho. Misc. Doc. No. 42, Part 8 (Washington, DC: GPO, 1884), 53.
30 Annual Report of Special Treasury Agent George R. Tingle, 1887, in *Seal and Salmon Fisheries and General Resources of Alaska*, Vol. 1 (Washington, DC: GPO, 1898), 199.
31 Report of Assistant Treasury Agent Joseph Murray, November 1, 1891, in *Seal and Salmon Fisheries and General Resources of Alaska*, Vol. 1 (Washington, DC: GPO, 1898), 297.
32 Thomas A. Bailey, "The North Pacific Sealing Convention of 1911," *Pacific Historical Review* (March 1935): 1.
33 "Beginning—A Historical Record of the Fabulous Pacific N.W. Sealing Fleet," *Marine Digest* (May 4, 1957): 9; Act of April 6, 1894 (28 Stat. 52).
34 Act of December 29, 1897 (30 Stat. 226).
35 Annual Report of Special Treasury Agent Charles J. Goff, 1890, in *Seal and Salmon Fisheries and General Resources of Alaska*, Vol. 1 (Washington, DC: GPO, 1898), 230; Annual Report of Special Treasury Agent William H. Williams, 1891, in *Seal and Salmon Fisheries and General Resources of Alaska*, Vol. 1 (Washington, DC: GPO, 1898), 286, 289; fur seal skin shipment certification, September 7, 1892, in *Seal and Salmon Fisheries and General Resources of Alaska*, Vol. 1 (Washington, DC: GPO, 1898), 349; Report of Joseph B. Crowley, Special Treasury Agent, for the year 1894, in *Seal and Salmon Fisheries and General Resources of Alaska*, Vol. 1 (Washington, DC: GPO, 1898), 456.
36 Act to protect the seal fisheries of Alaska, and for other purposes (36 Stat. 326).
37 Thomas A. Bailey, "The North Pacific Sealing Convention of 1911," *Pacific Historical Review* (March 1935): 1. The 1911 Sealing Convention was the first international treaty to protect a marine resource.

38 Walter I. Lembkey, "Fur-Seal Service in 1911," in Barton Warren Evermann, *Alaska Fisheries and Fur Industries in 1911*, Bureau of Fisheries Doc. No. 766 (Washington, DC: GPO, 1912), 89; Barton Warren Evermann, *Alaska Fishery and Fur Industries in 1912*, Bureau of Fisheries Doc. No. 780 (Washington, DC: GPO, 1913), 9-11, 74-78; Barton Warren Evermann, *Alaska Fisheries and Fur Industries in 1913*, Bureau of Fisheries Doc. No. 797 (Washington, DC: GPO, 1914), 10; Ward T. Bower and Henry D. Aller, *Alaska Fisheries and Fur Industries in 1914*, Bureau of Fisheries Doc. No. 819 (Washington, DC: GPO, 1915), 69-73; Ward T. Bower and Henry D. Aller, *Alaska Fisheries and Fur Industries in 1915*, Bureau of Fisheries Doc. No. 834 (Washington, DC: GPO, 1917), 69-70, 106; Ward T. Bower and Henry D. Aller, *Alaska Fisheries and Fur Industries in 1916*, Bureau of Fisheries Doc. No. 838 (Washington, DC: GPO, 1917), 81-82, 105; Ward T. Bower and Henry D. Aller, *Alaska Fisheries and Fur Industries in 1917*, Bureau of Fisheries Doc. No. 847 (Washington, DC: GPO, 1918), 71; Ward T. Bower, *Alaska Fisheries and Fur Industries in 1918*, Bureau of Fisheries Doc. No. 872 (Washington, DC: GPO, 1919), 78-79.

39 Ward T. Bower, *Alaska Fisheries and Fur Industries in 1919*, Bureau of Fisheries Doc. No. 891 (Washington, DC: GPO, 1920), 74-76.

40 Annual Report of the Commissioner of Fisheries to the Secretary of Commerce for the Fiscal Year Ended June 30, 1920 (Washington, DC: GPO, 1920), 57.

41 Ward T. Bower, *Alaska Fishery and Fur-Seal Industries in 1923*, Bureau of Fisheries Doc. No. 973 (Washington, DC: GPO, 1925), 111-128.

42 E. Lester Jones, Bureau of Fisheries, *Report of Alaska Investigations in 1914* (Washington, DC: GPO, 1915), 37-38.

43 Ward T. Bower and Henry D. Aller, *Alaska Fisheries and Fur Industries in 1917*, Bureau of Fishery Doc. No. 847 (Washington, DC: GPO, 1918), 71.

44 E. Lester Jones, Bureau of Fisheries, *Report of Alaska Investigations in 1914* (Washington, DC: GPO, 1915), 37-38.

45 Ward T. Bower, *Alaska Fishery and Fur-Seal Industries in 1928*, Bureau of Fisheries Doc. No. 1064 (Washington, DC: GPO, 1929), 297.

46 Ward T. Bower, *Alaska Fishery and Fur-Seal Industries in 1929*, Bureau of Fisheries Doc. No. 1086 (Washington, DC: GPO, 1930), 295-307; "*Penguin I* Sails for Grand Cayman," *Marine Digest* (July 13, 1957): 15.

47 Mark Kurlansky, *Cod: A Biography of the Fish That Changed the World* (New York: Penguin Books, 1997), 24-29.

48 Sen. Charles Sumner, in *Russian America*, 40th Cong., 2d sess., Ho. Ex. Doc. No. 177, Pt. I, 1868, pp. 184-185.

49 *Fishing Grounds of the North Pacific Ocean*, 42d Cong., 2d sess., 1872, Sen. Ex. Doc. No. 34, p. 7.

50 Sen. Charles Sumner, in *Russian America*, 40th Cong., 2d sess., Ho. Ex. Doc. No. 177, Pt. I, 1868, pp. 184-185.

51 William H. Dall, *Alaska and Its Resources* (Boston: Lee and Shepard, 1870), 483.

52 George Davidson in *Russian America*, 40th Cong., 2d sess., Ho. Ex. Doc. No. 177, Pt. I, 1868, pp. 254-256.

53 Ward T. Bower and Henry D. Aller, *Alaska Fisheries and Fur Industries in 1914*, Bureau of Fisheries Doc. No. 819 (Washington, DC: GPO, 1915), 54; Gordon P. Jones, "Cod Bangers to Alaska," *Alaska Sportsman* (March 1966): 8; John N. Cobb, *Pacific Cod Fisheries*, Appendix IV to *Report of the U.S. Commissioner of Fisheries for 1915*, Bureau of Fisheries Document No. 830 (Washington, DC: GPO, 1916), 44.

54 Ward T. Bower and Henry D. Aller, *Alaska Fisheries and Fur Industries in 1916*, Bureau of Fisheries Doc. No. 838 (Washington, DC: GPO, 1917), 68-69.

55 Ward T. Bower, *Alaska Fishery and Fur-Seal Industries in 1939*, Administrative Rept. No. 40 (Washington, DC: GPO, 1941), 154-155; "*C. A. Thayer* to Be Museum in San Francisco," *Marine Digest* (June 9, 1956): 10.

56 "*C. A. Thayer* to Be Museum in San Francisco," *Marine Digest* (June 9, 1956): 10.

57 John J. Brueggeman, Terrell C. Newby, and Richard A. Grotefendt, "Seasonal Abundance, Distribution and Population Characteristics of Blue Whales Reported in the 1917 to 1939 Catch Records of Two Alaska Whaling Stations," *Thirty-fifth Report of the International Whaling Commission* (1985), 405-411; HDR Alaska, Inc., *Akutan Airport Master Plan, Draft Preliminary Site Assessment* (May 2006), 7, http://dot.alaska.gov/creg/akutan/assets/AkutanEA_appH.pdf (accessed March 15, 2012).

CHAPTER 2

1 R. N. DeArmond, "Sitka to Ounalaska Mail: The Fur Seal Route," *Sea Chest* (June 1982): 119.

2 "Maritime Memories," *Marine Digest* (May 27, 1972): 23.

3 "Maritime Memories," *Marine Digest* (May 27, 1972): 23.

4 C. L. Andrews, "Mail Routes of the Northland," *Alaska Life* (April 1946): 20; J. Pennelope Goforth, *Sailing the Mail in Alaska* (Anchorage: Cybrrcat Productions, 2003), 19-33.

5 Thor Lauritzen, Peggy Arness, and Edward Melseth (compilers), *The Alaska Pen: An Illustrated History of Unga* (Bothell, Wash.: Book Publishers Network, 2007), 166; R. N. DeArmond, "Sitka to Ounalaska Mail: The Fur Seal Route," *Sea Chest* (June 1982): 119; "Maritime Memories," *Marine Digest* (May 27, 1972): 23.

6 Jay Ellis Ransom, "Life Was Simple at Umnak," *Alaska Sportsman* (September 1944): 14.

7 "Steamer *Starr* Arrives Here; Going Westward," *Alaska Daily Empire*, December 16, 1921.

8 Anthony Dimond, in *Powerboat Service for Alaska*, hearing, House Committee on the Post Office and Post Roads, June 30, 1939 (Washington, DC: GPO, 1939), 4.

9 John Barton Corson, "Alaska to the Rhine," privately printed in Auburn, California, in 1991, p. 108; "Alaska Co. Takes Over the *Starr*," *Marine Digest* (April 6, 1935): 3; "Steamer *Starr* Arrives Here; Going Westward," *Alaska Daily Empire*, December 16, 1921.

10 "Steamer *Starr* Arrives Here; Going Westward," *Alaska Daily Empire*, December 16, 1921.

11 John Barton Corson, "Alaska to the Rhine," privately printed in Auburn, California, in 1991, pp. 82, 86.

12 "Steamer *Starr* Arrives Here; Going Westward," *Alaska Daily Empire*, December 16, 1921.

13 Advertisement, *Marine Digest* (December 2, 1922): 6.

14 "SS *Starr* Passengers on This Voyage Are Few in Number," *Seward Gateway*, January 29, 1935.

15 John Barton Corson, "Alaska to the Rhine," privately printed in Auburn, California, in 1991, p. 92; Jay Ellis Ransom, "Life Was Simple at Umnak," *Alaska Sportsman* (September 1944): 14.

16 Carlyle Eubanks, Aleutian Livestock Co., in *Powerboat Service for Alaska*, hearing, House Committee on the Post Office and Post Roads, June 30, 1939 (Washington, DC: GPO, 1939), 15; John Barton Corson, "Alaska to the Rhine," privately printed in Auburn, California, in 1991, pp. 82, 88.

17 John Barton Corson, "Alaska to the Rhine," privately printed in Auburn, California, in 1991, pp. 78, 82, 85.

18 Arthur J. Harris, letter to publisher, *Alaska Life*, November 30, 1943, printed as Únalaska Letter, *Alaska Life* (April 1944): 44.

19 Jay Ellis Ransom, "Sheep Raising at Umnak," *Alaska Sportsman* (April 1939): 8; John Barton Corson, "Alaska to the Rhine," privately printed in Auburn, California, in 1991, p. 90; Arthur J. Harris, letter to publisher, *Alaska Life*, November 30, 1943, printed as Únalaska Letter, *Alaska Life* (April 1944): 44; Carlyle C. Eubanks, Aleutian Livestock Co., in *Powerboat Service for Alaska*, hearing, House Committee on the Post Office and Post Roads, June 30, 1939 (Washington, DC: GPO, 1939), 12.

20 John Barton Corson, "Alaska to the Rhine," privately printed in Auburn, California, in 1991, p. 97.

21 Carlyle C. Eubanks, Aleutian Livestock Co., in *Powerboat Service for Alaska*, hearing, House Committee on the Post Office and Post Roads, June 30, 1939 (Washington, DC: GPO, 1939), 14.

22 John Barton Corson, "Alaska to the Rhine," privately printed in Auburn, California, in 1991, p. 97.

23 John Barton Corson, "Alaska to the Rhine," privately printed in Auburn, California, in 1991, p. 95.

24 "*Starr* in Port with Passengers from Westward," *Seward Gateway*, May 9, 1935; "*Starr* Makes Quick Trip on the Westward Voyage," *Seward Gateway*, May 30, 1935.

25 William C. Redfield in *Centennial Celebration of the United States Coast and Geodetic Survey* (April 6, 1916), 132, reprinted in part in Ernest Gruening, *The State of Alaska* (New York: Random House, 1954), 221; see also: "U.S. Coast Survey Using Aged Ships," *New York Times*, December 4, 1914.

26 John Barton Corson, "Alaska to the Rhine," privately printed in Auburn, California, in 1991, p. 105.

27 Captain Lloyd H. "Kinky" Bayers collection, December 12, 1928, Alaska State Library, Historical Section.

28 Alonzo J. Moser, "The Race," in Lael Morgan, chief ed., *The Aleutians* (Vol. 7, No. 3, *Alaska Geographic*, 1980): 38-39.

29 "Alaska Co. Takes Over the *Starr*," *Marine Digest* (April 6, 1935): 3.

30 "The Grand Old SS *Starr*," *Seward Gateway*, April 23, 1935; "SS *Starr* Under New House Flag Arrives Port," *Seward Gateway*, April 20, 1935.

31 "Twins Are Born Westward Trip Steamer *Starr*," *Seward Gateway*, January 29, 1935.

32 "SS *Starr* Under New House Flag Arrives Port," *Seward Gateway*, April 20, 1935.

33 "*Starr* Coming for Overhaul," *Marine Digest* (February 15, 1936): 3.

34 Leon S. Vincent, "A Sailor for You!" *Alaska Sportsman* (March 1946): 8.

35 James A. Farley (Postmaster General) to Sen. Kenneth McKellar (chairman, Committee on Post Offices and Post Roads), in *Authorizing the Postmaster General to Contract for Certain Powerboat Service in Alaska*, 76th Cong., 1st sess., Sen. Rept. No. 955, July 26, 1939, p. 2.

36 Anthony Dimond, in *Powerboat Service for Alaska*, hearing, House Committee on the Post Office and Post Roads, June 30, 1939 (Washington, DC: GPO, 1939), 4.

37 October 28, 1922; April 6, 1935; February 15, 1936.

38 Carlyle C. Eubanks, Aleutian Livestock Co., in *Powerboat Service for Alaska*, hearing, House Committee on the Post Office and Post Roads, June 30, 1939 (Washington, DC: GPO, 1939), 13.

39 Alaska Traders to Collector of Customs, July 1, 1939, NARA, Pacific Alaska Region, RG 36, U.S. Customs Service, Box 11 06/03/10(5).

40 Anthony Dimond, in *Powerboat Service for Alaska*, hearing, House Committee on the Post Office and Post Roads, June 30, 1939 (Washington, DC: GPO, 1939), 4; American Bureau of Shipping, *The Record*, 1938; untitled document, NARA, Pacific Alaska Region, RG 36, U.S. Customs Service, Box 11 06/03/10(5).

41 Certificate of Inspection, July 17, 1940, NARA, Pacific Alaska Region, RG 36, U.S. Customs Service, Box 11 06/03/10(5).

42 Leon S. Vincent, "A Sailor for You!" *Alaska Sportsman* (March 1946): 8.

43 "Seattle C of C Succeeds in Securing Service to Aleutians," *Alaska Life* (May 1940): 16.

44 Carlyle Eubanks, Aleutian Livestock Co., in *Powerboat Service for Alaska*, hearing, House Committee on the Post Office and Post Roads, June 30, 1939 (Washington, DC: GPO, 1939), 15.

45 *Congressional Record*, House, 10963, August 3, 1939.

46 Act of August 10, 1939 (76 Stat. 1338).

47 Certificate of Inspection, July 17, 1940, NARA, Pacific Alaska Region, RG 36, U.S. Customs Service, Box 11 06/03/10(5).

48 NARA, Pacific Alaska Region, RG 36, U.S. Customs Service, Box 11 06/03/10(5).

49 "Missing Craft Turns Up at Dutch Harbor," *Marine Digest* (February 19, 1966): 36.

CHAPTER 3

1 Providing for Ocean Transportation Service to and from Alaska Until March 1, 1949, 80th Cong., 2d sess., 1948, Sen. Rept. No. 1755, p. 1.

2 80th Cong., 2d sess., *Transportation in Alaska*, H. Rept. No. 1272 (Washington, DC: GPO, 1948), 11.

3 Providing for Ocean Transportation Service to and from Alaska Until March 1, 1949, 80th Cong., 2d sess., 1948, Sen. Rept. No. 1755, p. 2.

4 S. G. Hayman, "A Cargo Handling Revolution," *Marine Digest* (April 27, 1957): 7.

5 "Alaska Steamship Celebrates 65th Year," *Marine Digest* (March 5, 1960): 7.

6 "Another Attack by Gruening" (editorial), *Marine Digest* (February 6, 1960): 4.

7 "Alaska Log," *Marine Digest* (May 7, 1966): 9.

8 Ward T. Bower, *Alaska Fishery and Fur-Seal Industries: 1943* (Washington, DC: GPO, 1944), 40-41.

9 Ward T. Bower, *Alaska Fishery and Fur-Seal Industries: 1943* (Washington, DC: GPO, 1944), 40-41; Ward T. Bower, *Alaska Fishery and Fur-Seal Industries: 1948, Statistical Digest No. 15* (Washington, DC: GPO, 1948), 46; Ward T. Bower, *Alaska Fishery and Fur-Seal Industries: 1948, Statistical Digest No. 17* (Washington, DC: GPO, 1948), 51; Seton H. Thompson, *Alaska Fishery and Fur-Seal Industries: 1947, Statistical Digest No. 20* (Washington, DC: GPO, 1950), 56-57; Seton H. Thompson, *Alaska Fishery and Fur-Seal Industries: 1948, Statistical Digest No. 23* (Washington, DC: GPO, 1952), 46-47; Seton H. Thompson, *Alaska Fishery and Fur-Seal Industries: 1949, Statistical Digest No. 26* (Washington, DC: GPO, 1952), 58; Seton H. Thompson, *Alaska Fishery and Fur-Seal Industries: 1950, Statistical Digest No. 29* (Washington, DC: GPO, 1953), 54; "*Penguin II* Sails Pribilof Islands Run," Dept. of the Interior, news release, September 26, 1950.

10 "Ship Loads First of Pribilof Skins," *Marine Digest* (February 22, 1964): 36.

11 "Aleut Corp. Purchases Ocean Vessel," *Anchorage Times*, no date.

12 "No More Export Declarations on Alaskan and Hawaiian Shipments," *Pacific Marine Review* (May 1948): 76.

13 L. Wakefield to stockholders, August 11, 1947, in Mansel G. Blackford, *Pioneering a Modern Small Business: Wakefield Seafoods and the Alaskan Frontier* (Greenwich, Conn.: Jai Press, 1979), 14.

14 Mansel G. Blackford, *Pioneering a Modern Small Business: Wakefield Seafoods and the Alaskan Frontier* (Greenwich, Conn.: Jai Press, 1979), 19.

15 Ward T. Bower, *Alaska Fishery and Fur-Seal Industries in 1937* (Washington, DC: GPO, 1938), 75.

16 Russell Nelson, Jr., Robert French, and Janet Wall, "Sampling by U.S. Observers on Foreign Fishing Vessels in the Eastern Bering Sea and Aleutian Island Region, 1977-78," *Marine Fisheries Review* (May 1981): 1.

17 Thor Lauritzen, Peggy Arness, and Edward Melseth (compilers), *The Alaska Pen: An Illustrated History of Unga* (Bothell, Wash.: Book Publishers Network, 2007), 169, 171.

18 Advertisement, *Marine Digest* (September 2, 1950): 2.

19 "*Aleutian Mail* Under Tow; All Are Saved," *Seward Polaris & Kenai Peninsula-Aleutian Chain News* (January 14, 1948); "Coast Guard Inadequate; Congress Must Be at Fault," *Seward Polaris & Kenai Peninsula-Aleutian Chain News* (January 28, 1948); "*Aleutian Mail* Will Go to Seattle," *Seward Polaris & Kenai Peninsula-Aleutian Chain News* (January 17, 1948); Thor Lauritzen, Peggy Arness, and Edward Melseth (compilers), *The Alaska Pen: An Illustrated History of Unga* (Bothell, Wash.: Book Publishers Network, 2007), 115, 171-172.

20 "Contract Annulled *Aleutian Mail*," *Seward Polaris & Kenai Peninsula-Aleutian Chain News* (March 3, 1948); Thor Lauritzen, Peggy Arness, and Edward Melseth (compilers), *The Alaska Pen: An Illustrated History of Unga* (Bothell, Wash.: Book Publishers Network, 2007), 172.

21 Thor Lauritzen, Peggy Arness, and Edward Melseth (compilers), *The Alaska Pen: An Illustrated History of Unga* (Bothell, Wash.: Book Publishers Network, 2007), 173-174.

22 Thor Lauritzen, Peggy Arness, and Edward Melseth (compilers), *The Alaska Pen: An Illustrated History of Unga* (Bothell, Wash.: Book Publishers

Network, 2007), 175; "Boat Mail Service to West Is Awarded Berger," *Daily Alaska Empire*, March 30, 1949.

23 "First Mailboat to Westward Sails Saturday," *Seward Seaport Record*, April 22, 1949; American Bureau of Shipping, *The Record*, 1953.

24 "Heinie Berger Dead in Seattle," *Seward Seaport Record*, January 29, 1954; advertisement, *Seward Gateway* (November 20, 1934); "*Discoverer* on Last Trip of Season South," *Seward Gateway*, November 22, 1934; *Heinie Berger et al., Appellants, v. Sailors Union of the Pacific et al.*, 29 Wn.2d 810 [No. 30277. En Banc. Supreme Court February 13, 1948].

25 R. H. Calkins, "E. J. (Gene) Townsend Operates Far-Flung Alaska Service," *Marine Digest* (April 10, 1954): 4; "First Mailboat to Westward Sails Saturday," *Seward Seaport Record*, April 22, 1949.

26 "Boat Mail Service to West Is Awarded Berger," *Daily Alaska Empire*, March 30, 1949; R. H. Calkins, "E. J. (Gene) Townsend Operates Far-Flung Alaska Service," *Marine Digest* (April 10, 1954): 4.

27 R. H. Calkins, "E. J. (Gene) Townsend Operates Far-Flung Alaska Service," *Marine Digest* (April 10, 1954): 28.

28 R. H. Calkins, "E. J. (Gene) Townsend Operates Far-Flung Alaska Service," *Marine Digest* (April 10, 1954): 4.

29 Thor Lauritzen, Peggy Arness, and Edward Melseth (compilers), *The Alaska Pen: An Illustrated History of Unga* (Bothell, Wash.: Book Publishers Network, 2007), 175.

30 *Contracting for Mail-Boat Service in Alaska*, Ho. Committee on Post Office and Civil Service, 86th Cong., 2d sess., May 6, 1960 (Washington, DC: GPO, 1960), 5. Quoting Raymond J. Peterson, attorney for Kimbrell-Lawrence Transportation, Inc.

31 Angus Whyte, former employee, Kimbrell-Lawrence Transportation, Inc., personal communication with author, July 9, 2008.

32 Anna Martin, *Around and About Alaska* (New York: Vantage Press, 1959), 82-94.

33 *Contracting for Mail-Boat Service in Alaska*, Ho. Committee on Post Office and Civil Service, 86th Cong., 2d sess., May 6, 1960 (Washington, DC: GPO, 1960), 8. Quoting Raymond J. Peterson, attorney for Kimbrell-Lawrence Transportation, Inc.

34 R. H. Calkins, "E. J. (Gene) Townsend Operates Far-Flung Alaska Service," *Marine Digest* (April 10, 1954): 4.

35 American Bureau of Shipping, *The Record*, 1958; Gordon Newell, ed., *H. W. McCurdy Marine History of the Pacific Northwest* (Seattle: Superior Publishing Co., 1966), 602; "Expansion Takes Over," *Mailboat Monitor* (Seward), June 1956; "New Service Set Seattle-Alaska," *Marine Digest* (June 3, 1961): 2.

36 Advertisement, *Marine Digest* (October 1, 1955): no page; advertisement, *Marine Digest* (March 3, 1956): 12.

37 Tommy Corr, "A Land of Sheep," *Alaska Sportsman* (April 1959): 14.

38 *Contracting for Mail-Boat Service in Alaska*, Ho. Committee on Post Office and Civil Service, 86th Cong., 2d sess., May 6, 1960 (Washington, DC: GPO, 1960), 5. Quoting Raymond J. Peterson, attorney for Kimbrell-Lawrence Transportation, Inc.; Gale Blaisingame, formerly with Wash. Fish & Oyster, personal communication with author, February 26, 2008.

39 Robert E. Dignon, Northern Products Corp., letter to Sen. Ernest Gruening in *Inspection of Certain Small Vessels Carrying Freight*, February 16, 1960, H. Merchant Marine and Fisheries Subcommittee, 86th Cong., 2d sess. (Washington, DC: GPO, 1960), 2.

40 "Alaska Line May Have to Withdraw Freezer Vessels," *Marine Digest* (April 10, 1954): 4; "Alaska Line to Retain *Palisana, Lucidor* on Run," *Marine Digest* (April 17, 1954): 3.

41 Gordon Newell, ed., *H. W. McCurdy Marine History of the Pacific Northwest* (Seattle: Superior Publishing Co., 1966), 465; John Barton Corson, "Alaska to the Rhine," privately printed in Auburn, California, in 1991, p. 95.

42 Robert J. Cressman, "YAG-11 *Baranof*," *Dictionary of American Naval Fighting Ships*, http://www.hazegray.org/danfs (accessed June 16, 2009).

43 "Shipping News," *Seward Seaport Record*, October 16, 1948, and October 23, 1948.

44 "*Western Pioneer* Sails Rugged Alaska Route," *Marine Digest* (August 31, 1963): 12.

45 Gale Blaisingame, formerly with Wash. Fish & Oyster, personal communication with author, February 26, 2008.

46 Gordon Newell, ed., *H. W. McCurdy Marine History of the Pacific Northwest* (Seattle: Superior Publishing Co., 1966), 652.

47 "Little Wood Ship Defies Alaska's Stormy Seas," *Alaska Industry* (July 1969): 26; *Contracting for Mail-Boat Service in Alaska*, Ho. Committee on Post Office

and Civil Service, 86th Cong., 2d sess., May 6, 1960 (Washington, DC: GPO, 1960), 5. Quoting Raymond J. Peterson, attorney for Kimbrell-Lawrence Transportation, Inc.

48 *Contracting for Mail-Boat Service in Alaska*, Ho. Committee on Post Office and Civil Service, 86th Cong., 2d sess., May 6, 1960 (Washington, DC: GPO, 1960), 5-6. Quoting Raymond J. Peterson, attorney for Kimbrell-Lawrence Transportation, Inc.

49 American Bureau of Shipping, *The Record*, 1964; "Kimbrell-Lawrence Moves to New Quarters," *Marine Digest* (November 5, 1960): 51-52.

50 Gordon Newell, ed., *H. W. McCurdy Marine History of the Pacific Northwest* (Seattle: Superior Publishing Co., 1966), 626; *Contracting for Mail-Boat Service in Alaska*, Ho. Committee on Post Office and Civil Service, 86th Cong., 2d sess., May 6, 1960 (Washington, DC: GPO, 1960), 6. Quoting Raymond J. Peterson, attorney for Kimbrell-Lawrence Transportation, Inc.; Angus Whyte, former employee, Kimbrell-Lawrence Transportation, Inc., personal communication with author, October 10, 2008.

51 *Contracting for Mail-Boat Service in Alaska*, Ho. Committee on Post Office and Civil Service, 86th Cong., 2d sess., May 6, 1960 (Washington, DC: GPO, 1960), 5. Quoting Raymond J. Peterson, attorney for Kimbrell-Lawrence Transportation, Inc.; "Kimbrell-Lawrence Moves to New Quarters," *Marine Digest* (November 5, 1960): 51-52.

52 "Kimbrell-Lawrence Moves to New Quarters," *Marine Digest* (November 5, 1960): 51-52.

53 Ed L. Kimbrell to Federal Maritime Board, November 19, 1958, in *Restricting the Route of Certain Mail-Boat Service in Alaska*, Ho. Committee on Post Office and Civil Service, 86th Cong., 1st sess., July 8, 1959 (Washington, DC: GPO, 1959), 14.

54 *Contracting for Mail-Boat Service in Alaska*, Ho. Committee on Post Office and Civil Service, 86th Cong., 2d sess., May 6, 1960 (Washington, DC: GPO, 1960), 5, 6. Quoting Raymond J. Peterson, attorney for Kimbrell-Lawrence Transportation, Inc.; "Pioneer Alaska Line Offers Unique Service," *Marine Digest* (May 3, 1969): 12.

55 Ed L. Kimbrell to Federal Maritime Board, November 19, 1958, in *Restricting the Route of Certain Mailboat Service*

in *Alaska*, Ho. Committee on Post Office and Civil Service, 86th Cong., 1st sess., July 8, 1959 (Washington, DC: GPO, 1959), 14; "Kimbrell-Lawrence Moves to New Quarters," *Marine Digest* (November 5, 1960): 51-52.

56 "Hearing Held on Alaska Rates," *Marine Digest* (February 15, 1958): 1.

57 "Refrigerator-Van Service Increased," *Marine Digest* (November 2, 1957): 8.

58 "Loss of Fish Cargo Seen as Problem," *Marine Digest* (September 21, 1957): 2.

59 B. E. Gilman, Vita Food Products, in *Inspection of Certain Small Vessels Carrying Freight*, February 16, 1960, H. Merchant Marine and Fisheries Subcommittee, 86th Cong., 2d sess. (Washington, DC: GPO, 1960), 5; W. B. Hall, Booth Fisheries, in *Inspection of Certain Small Vessels Carrying Freight*, February 16, 1960, H. Merchant Marine and Fisheries Subcommittee, 86th Cong., 2d sess. (Washington, DC: GPO, 1960), 3.

60 "Commendation Is Given by USCG," *Marine Digest* (February 13, 1960): 9.

61 "Commendation Is Given by USCG," *Marine Digest* (February 13, 1960): 9.

62 Exec. Order No. 9472, August 29, 1944 (46 C.F.R. 39, §2003).

63 "*Western Pioneer* Wins Gallant Ship Award," *Marine Digest* (July 15, 1961): 24.

64 USMM.org, Gallant Ships of World War II Merchant Marine, http://www.usmm.org/gallantships.html (accessed July 5, 2008).

65 "Aleutian Mail Run Starts Controversy," *Marine Digest* (March 14, 1959): 2.

66 Senate Joint Memorial No. 3, *Laws of Alaska*, 1959, p. 387.

67 "Aleutian Mail Run Starts Controversy," *Marine Digest* (March 14, 1959): 2.

68 "Bids Opened for New Alaska Ship Mail Run," *Marine Digest* (May 9, 1959): 2.

69 "Bid Award Awaited on Alaska Mail Contract," *Marine Digest* (July 11, 1959): 6.

70 S. 1849.

71 *Operation Route of Postal Powerboat Service in Alaska*, H. Rept. No. 1921, 86th Cong., 2d sess., 1960, pp. 2, 3.

72 "New Service Set Seattle-Alaska," *Marine Digest* (June 3, 1961): 2; "Office Open for Aleutian Marine," *Marine Digest* (August 12, 1961): 40; advertisement, *Marine Digest* (July 8, 1961): 18.

73 "Aleutian Mail Boat Service to Continue," *Marine Digest* (March 10, 1962): 46.

74 Advertisement, *Marine Digest* (November 16, 1963): 12.

75 Niels Peter Thomsen, *Voyage of the Forest Dream* (Vancouver, Wash.: Rose Wind Press, 1997), 158.

76 Niels Peter Thomsen, *Voyage of the Forest Dream* (Vancouver, Wash.: Rose Wind Press, 1997), 116; Carl Moses, Aleutian Islands area businessman, personal communication with author, August 5, 2008.

CHAPTER 4

1 Angus Whyte, former employee, Kimbrell-Lawrence Transportation, Inc., personal communication with author, July 9, 2008.

2 "Kimbrell-Lawrence Moves to New Quarters," *Marine Digest* (November 5, 1960): 51-52.

3 "Pioneer Alaska Line Offers Unique Service," *Marine Digest* (May 3, 1969): 12.

4 46 U.S.C. 883.

5 Angus Whyte, former employee, Kimbrell-Lawrence Transportation, Inc., personal communication with author, October 5, 2008.

6 "*Western Pioneer* Loads at NSD for Alaska," *Marine Digest* (July 15, 1961): 40.

7 "*Western Pioneer* Sails Rugged Alaska Route," *Marine Digest* (August 31, 1963): 12.

8 "Expansion Set by Kimbrell-Lawrence," *Marine Digest* (April 8, 1967): 3; "*Western Pioneer* Sails Rugged Alaska Route," *Marine Digest* (August 31, 1963): 12; Angus Whyte, former employee, Kimbrell-Lawrence Transportation, Inc., personal communication with author, July 14, 2008.

9 "*Western Pioneer* Does Much Damage," *Marine Digest* (January 19, 1963): 26.

10 "*Western Pioneer* Sails Rugged Alaska Route," *Marine Digest* (August 31, 1963): 12.

11 Angus Whyte, former employee, Kimbrell-Lawrence Transportation, Inc., personal communication with author, July 11, 2008.

12 "*Western Pioneer* Sails Rugged Alaska Route," *Marine Digest* (August 31, 1963): 12.

13 John J. Wheatley and Guy G. Gordon, *Economic and Transport Developments in Alaska's Future* (Seattle: Graduate School of Business Administration, University of Washington, 1969), 151; U.S. Federal Maritime Commission, Bureau of Domestic Regulation, Alaska Trade Study (Washington, DC: GPO, July 1967), III-6.

14 Angus Whyte, former employee, Kimbrell-Lawrence Transportation, Inc., personal communication with author, July 21, 2008.

15 Angus Whyte, former employee, Kimbrell-Lawrence Transportation, Inc., personal communication with author, July 21, 2008.

16 "Kimbrell-Lawrence Adds Depue to Staff," *Marine Digest* (September 4, 1965): 8.

17 Angus Whyte, former employee, Kimbrell-Lawrence Transportation, Inc., personal communication with author, July 14, 2008.

18 "Expansion Set by Kimbrell-Lawrence," *Marine Digest* (April 8, 1967): 3.

19 "Pan-Alaska Moves Ahead with 3 New Plants," *Pacific Fisherman* (October 1966): 14.

20 *Unalaskan*, June 23, 1969.

21 Angus Whyte, former employee, Kimbrell-Lawrence Transportation, Inc., personal communication with author, February 18, 2009; Larry Soriano, president, Western Pioneer, Inc., personal communication with author, February 19, 2009.

22 Scott Loners, former employee, Western Pioneer, Inc., personal communication with author, February 18, 2009.

23 Resource Inventory for the Aleutians East Coastal Resource Service Area (1984), Appendix B to Aleutians East Borough Coastal Management Plan (January 2008), Ch. 13, p. 25.

24 Carl Moses, former Alaska legislator, personal communication with author, October 30, 2008.

25 FY 1975 Alaska Legislature Free Conference Committee Report, Operating and Capital Budget.

26 "Marine Intelligence," *Marine Digest* (February 19, 1949): 5.

27 Angus Whyte, former employee, Kimbrell-Lawrence Transportation, Inc., personal communication with author, February 18, 2009.

28 "SS *Oduna* Total Loss on Unimak Island," *Marine Digest* (December 4, 1965): 2; "SS *Oduna* Salvage Work Is Reported," *Marine Digest* (December 18, 1965): 3; "Crab Containers Taken from Wrecked Ship," *Marine Digest* (January 1, 1966): 39.

29 "MS *Polar Pioneer* Has New Bow Thrusters," *Marine Digest* (July 1, 1967): 3; "Freezer Vessel Conversion Completed," *Marine Digest* (August 26, 1972): 33.

30 "Expansion Set by Kimbrell-Lawrence," *Marine Digest* (April 8, 1967): 3.

31 "*Polar Pioneer* Sets First Voyage July 3," *Marine Digest* (June 24, 1967): 2.

32 "*Polar Pioneer* Gets Good Seattle Sendoff," *Marine Digest* (July 8, 1967): 2.

33 "*Western Pioneer* Last of Wooden Freighters," *Marine Digest* (January 11, 1969): 18.

34 "Little Wood Ship Defies Alaska's Stormy Seas," *Alaska Industry* (July 1969): 26;

"*Western Pioneer* Back After Mishap in BC," *Marine Digest* (April 27, 1968): 10; "New Ship Colors," *Marine Digest* (July 19, 1969): 5; "*Western Pioneer* Sails Rugged Alaska Route," *Marine Digest* (August 31, 1963): 12; "Pioneer Alaska Line Offers Unique Service," *Marine Digest* (May 3, 1969): 12.

35 Don Page, *Seattle Post-Intelligencer*, February 8, 1969 (from Captain Lloyd H. "Kinky" Bayers collection, Alaska State Library, Historical Section).

36 "Kimbrell to Head Search for Queen," *Marine Digest* (April 13, 1968): 3.

37 Angus Whyte, former employee, Kimbrell-Lawrence Transportation, Inc., personal communication with author, July 14, 2008.

38 Frank Buckler, Jr., personal communication with author, Lynnwood, Wash., May 2008; Angus Whyte, former employee, Kimbrell-Lawrence Transportation, Inc., personal communication with author, July 9, 2008.

39 "Little Wood Ship Defies Alaska's Stormy Seas," *Alaska Industry* (July 1969): 26.

40 Linne Bardarson, formerly of the New England Fish Co., personal communication with author, February 10, 2008.

41 Advertisement, Kimbrell-Lawrence Transportation, *Marine Digest* (February 7, 1970).

42 Gordon Newell, ed., *H. W. McCurdy Marine History of the Pacific Northwest, 1966 to 1976* (Seattle: Superior Publishing Co., 1977), 94.

43 "Alaska Steamship Co. to Close Its Doors," *Marine Digest* (January 23, 1971): 3; "Ode to the Alaska Line," *Marine Digest* (January 30, 1971): 7.

44 "Alaska Steamship Co. to Close Its Doors," *Marine Digest* (January 23, 1971): 3; Sea-Land Service advertisement, *Marine Digest* (May 9, 1964): no page.

45 "MS *Polar Pioneer* Sold to Rados Western," *Marine Digest* (October 2, 1971): 3.

46 Angus Whyte, former employee, Kimbrell-Lawrence Transportation, Inc., personal communication with author, July 14, 2008.

47 Ted Choat (student), *Unalaskan*, May 19, 1970.

48 *Pan-Alaska Fisheries, Inc. v. Kimbrell-Lawrence Transportation, Inc.*, brief of Appellee to Ninth Circuit Court of Appeals.

49 Gordon Newell, ed., *H. W. McCurdy Marine History of the Pacific Northwest, 1966 to 1976* (Seattle: Superior

Publishing Co., 1977), 81.

50 Angus Whyte, former employee, Kimbrell-Lawrence Transportation, Inc., personal communication with author, July 14, 2008.

51 Angus Whyte, former employee, Kimbrell-Lawrence Transportation, Inc., personal communication with author, November 3, 2008.

CHAPTER 5

1 Amigo Soriano, former president, Western Pioneer, Inc., personal communications with author, 2007-2008.

2 Greg Larson, Puget Sound pilot and former Western Pioneer, Inc., captain, personal communication with author, March 9, 2008.

3 R. H. Calkins, "Capt. Rupert James Soriano; Four Brothers Officers in Same Ship," Chapter CCCVI of "Captains of the Pacific Northwest Maritime Industry," in *Marine Digest* (February 1, 1958): 5.

4 Karl House, Puget Sound Maritime Historical Society, personal communication with author.

5 Tyler Caruso, former port captain, Western Pioneer, Inc., personal communication with author, March 17, 2008; Tom Boyer, "Working Waterfront Losing a Mainstay," *Seattle Times*, June 25, 2005; Angus Whyte, former president, Alaska Marine Shipping, personal communication with author, November 3, 2008.

6 Larry Soriano, president, Western Pioneer, Inc., personal communication with author, January 9, 2009; Scott Loners, former employee, Western Pioneer, Inc., personal communication with author, June 13, 2008.

7 Scott Loners, former employee, Western Pioneer, Inc., personal communication with author, June 13, 2008.

8 Angus Whyte, former president, Alaska Marine Shipping, personal communication with author, March 5, 2009.

9 Larry Soriano, president, Western Pioneer, Inc., personal communication with author, March 4, 2009.

10 Scott Loners, former employee, Western Pioneer, Inc., personal communication with author, June 13, 2008.

11 Pub. L. No. 90-397, 82 Stat. 341 (1968).

12 Christopher L. Koch, "Regulation of the Use and Operation of Vessels Engaged in the Fisheries and Coastwise Trade of the United States" (unpublished), 1983.

13 Angus Whyte, former president,

Alaska Marine Shipping, personal communication with author, July 31, 2008.

CHAPTER 6

1 L. E. Burd, Alaska Marine Charters, Inc., to George C. Silides, undated, in Harold H. Galliet, Jr., and George C. Silides, *Port and Vessel Study: Extension of the Marine Highway System*, Vol. V, prepared for the Division of Marine Transportation, State of Alaska, November 1976, Appendix.

2 Angus Whyte, former president, Alaska Marine Shipping, personal communication with author, July 31, 2008.

3 Angus Whyte, former president, Alaska Marine Shipping, personal communication with author, February 8, 2009.

4 Angus Whyte, former president, Alaska Marine Shipping, personal communication with author, March 5, 2009.

5 Carl Moses, former president, Aleut Corp., personal communication with author, June 25, 2008.

6 Angus Whyte, former president, Alaska Marine Shipping, personal communication with author, July 11, 2008.

7 Harold H. Galliet, Jr., and George C. Silides, *Port and Vessel Study: Extension of the Marine Highway System*, Vol. V, prepared for the Division of Marine Transportation, State of Alaska, November 1976, p. 72.

8 *Aleutian Current* (Aleut Corp. newsletter), October 1975.

9 "Aleut Corp. Purchases Ocean Vessel," *Anchorage Times*, no date; Carl Moses, former president, Aleut Corp., personal communication with author, June 25, 2008.

10 Angus Whyte, former president, Alaska Marine Shipping, personal communication with author, July 11, 2008.

11 *Aleutian Current* (Aleut Corp. newsletter), February 1976.

12 Carl Moses, former president, Aleut Corp., personal communication with author, June 25, 2008.

13 *Aleutian Current* (Aleut Corp. newsletter), April 1977.

14 Dennis Heeney, former financial officer, Alaska Marine Shipping, personal communication with author, July 11, 2008.

15 *Aleutian Current* (Aleut Corp. newsletter), November 1977; Angus

Whyte, former president, Alaska Marine Shipping, personal communication with author, February 8, 2009.

16 Dennis Heeney, former financial officer, Alaska Marine Shipping, personal communication with author, July 11, 2008.

17 Angus Whyte, former president, Alaska Marine Shipping, personal communication with author, August 2, 2008.

18 Harold H. Galliet, Jr., and George C. Silides, *Port and Vessel Study: Extension of the Marine Highway System*, Vol. V, prepared for the Division of Marine Transportation, State of Alaska, November 1976, p. 72.

19 Angus Whyte, former president, Alaska Marine Shipping, personal communication with author, August 21, 2008, p. 72.

20 Robert Browning, "Bairdi Abundance May Alter with Sea Temperature," *National Fisherman* (August 1979): 4.

21 Harold H. Galliet, Jr., and George C. Silides, *Port and Vessel Study: Extension of the Marine Highway System*, Vol. V, prepared for the Division of Marine Transportation, State of Alaska, November 1976, p. 84.

22 "*Pvt. Frank Petrarca* on Seattle Adak Run," *Marine Digest* (April 15, 1972): 24; "Sea-Land Takes Position," *Aleutian Eagle*, July 20, 1990.

23 Harold H. Galliet, Jr., and George C. Silides, *Port and Vessel Study: Extension of the Marine Highway System*, Vol. V, prepared for the Division of Marine Transportation, State of Alaska, November 1976, p. 97.

24 "Aleutian Developer Enters Alaska Trade," *Marine Digest* (December 20, 1975): 11; Harold H. Galliet, Jr., and George C. Silides, *Port and Vessel Study: Extension of the Marine Highway System*, Vol. V, prepared for the Division of Marine Transportation, State of Alaska, November 1976, p. 97; John Gray, "Alaska's Unique Transportation System," *Alaska Review of Social and Economic Conditions* (June 1980): 1.

25 FY 1975 Alaska Legislature Free Conference Committee Report, Operating and Capital Budget; Harold H. Galliet, Jr., and George C. Silides, *Port and Vessel Study: Extension of the Marine Highway System*, Vol. V, prepared for the Division of Marine Transportation, State of Alaska, November 1976, p. 29.

26 FY 1975 Alaska Legislature Free Conference Committee Report,

Operating and Capital Budget.

27 Harold H. Galliet, Jr., and George C. Silides, *Port and Vessel Study: Extension of the Marine Highway System*, Vol. V, prepared for the Division of Marine Transportation, State of Alaska, November 1976, p. 94.

28 Carl Moses, purchaser of *Western Pioneer*, personal communication with author, April 24, 2008.

29 Anthony Olson, former captain, *Western Pioneer*, personal communication with author, May 23, 2008.

CHAPTER 7

1 Greg Larson, former captain, Western Pioneer, Inc., personal communication with author, March 9, 2008.

2 Angus Whyte, former president, Alaska Marine Shipping, personal communication with author, July 31, 2008, and July 23, 2009.

3 George Collazo, port captain, Coastal Transportation, Inc., personal communication with author, June 20, 2008.

4 33 CFR 95.020.

CHAPTER 8

1 Ward T. Bower, *Alaska Fisheries and Fur-Seal Industries in 1937* (Washington, DC: GPO, 1938), 75; Russell Nelson, Jr., Robert French, and Janet Wall, "Sampling by U.S. Observers on Foreign Fishing Vessels in the Eastern Bering Sea and Aleutian Island Region, 1977-78," *Marine Fisheries Review* (May 1981): 1.

2 "200 Mile Limit Asked," *Marine Digest* (June 13, 1970): 33.

3 "Fishboats Tied Up in Protest of Foreigners," *Marine Digest* (September 5, 1970): 6.

4 "Ship Seizures Focus World's Attention on 200-Mile Limit," *Pacific Fisherman* (January 1955): 42.

5 John Wiese, "Fisheries Treaty May Be in Trouble," *Alaska Industry* (June 1970): 45.

6 "Dear Colleague" letter by Senators John Tower, Dewey Bartlett, Dick Clark, Gale McGee, Hugh Scott, Robert Griffin, Strom Thurmond, and Barry Goldwater, January 19, 1976 ("200-Mile Bill Approved," in *A Legislative History of the Fishery Conservation and Management Act of 1976*, 94th Cong., 2d sess. (Washington, DC: GPO, 1976), 515.

7 Act of October 14, 1966, Establishing a Contiguous Fishery Zone Beyond the Territorial Sea of the United States (P.L. 89-658); "No More Deals" (editorial), *Marine Digest* (September 3, 1966): 8.

8 John Wiese, "Fisheries Treaty May Be in Trouble," *Alaska Industry* (June 1970): 45.

9 "Egan on Coast Limit," *Marine Digest* (September 2, 1972): 25.

10 "Fishing Fleet Hits High," *Marine Digest* (February 23, 1974): 38.

11 "The 200 Mile Limit," *Wall Street Journal*, December 8, 1975.

12 "The Fishing Bill," *Washington Post*, November 4, 1975.

13 "The Fishing Bill," *Washington Post*, November 4, 1975.

14 Fishery Conservation and Management Act of 1976, (P.L. 94-265).

15 George Rogers, personal communication with author, Juneau, Alaska, January 29, 2008.

16 Clem Tillion, in proceedings of the conference "Alaska Pollock: Is It a Red Herring?" sponsored by the Alaska Fisheries Development Foundation, Alaska Office of Commercial Fisheries Development, and National Marine Fisheries Service (Anchorage, January 1982), 6.

17 "Sea-Land's Hiltzheimer Convention Speaker," *Marine Digest* (July 27, 1974): 15.

18 Kim Suelzle, former manager, Icicle Seafoods, personal communication with author, March 10, 2008.

19 Alfred D. Chandler, " 'Fresh' or Frozen: Bottom Fish of the Bering Sea Bring Changes to the Fisherman," *Oceans* (November-December 1980): 22.

20 "Bottomfish: The Fishery of the Future?" *Pacific Fishing* (May 1980): 18.

21 Fishery Conservation and Management Act of 1976 (P.L. 94-265), § 3.

22 Grant Winthrop, "U.S. Fishermen Gear Up for a Haul Off Alaska," *Fortune* (January 29, 1979): 52, quoting Thomas A. Fulham, of Fulham and Maloney Co., Inc., a Boston fish company; Paul Clark, "No Fish Story: Sandwich Saved His McDonald's," *Cincinnati Enquirer*, February 20, 2007.

23 Michael J. Scott, "Prospects for a Bottomfish Industry in Alaska," *Alaska Review of Social and Economic Conditions* (April 1980): 8, 9, 12.

24 "Frozen Fish Business Has Made Its Own Luck," *Pacific Fisherman* (January 1966): 1.

25 "Bottomfish: The Fishery of the Future?" *Pacific Fishing* (May 1980): 18; J. Anthony Koslow, "Anatomy of a Modern Fishery: The Bering Sea Pollock Fishery," *Marine Technology Society Journal* (January 1976): 28.

26 John Gray, "Alaska's Unique Transportation System," *Alaska Review of Social and Economic Conditions* (June 1980): 1;

American President Lines advertisement, *National Fisherman* (April 30, 1980): 163.

27 Kenneth S. Hilderbrand (Oregon St. Univ.), *Model White Fish Project: Trident Seafoods, Akutan, Alaska, 1982/1985* (for the Alaska Fisheries Development Foundation), 1986, pp. 4-6; A. D. Chandler, "Alaska Companies Gear Up for Salt Cod," *National Fisherman* (March 1982): 10.

28 Kenneth S. Hilderbrand (Oregon St. Univ.), *Model White Fish Project: Trident Seafoods, Akutan, Alaska, 1982/1985* (for the Alaska Fisheries Development Foundation), 1986, p. 7.

29 Glenn Boledovich, "Trident Akutan Plant Burns," *Aleutian Eagle*, June 15, 1983; J. P. Goforth, "Trident Seafoods Rebuilds Akutan Plant," *Aleutian Eagle*, February 1, 1984; Krys Holmes, "Lodestar Update," *Aleutian Eagle*, December 27, 1984.

30 "Johansen Closes", *Aleutian Eagle*, April 1, 1983; survey in *Aleutian Times*, October 1984.

31 "Cargo Carriers Pull Out," *Aleutian Eagle*, February 15, 1983.

32 Angus Whyte, former president, Alaska Marine Shipping, personal communication with author, February 8, 2009.

33 Angus Whyte, former president, Alaska Marine Shipping, personal communication with author, October 7, 2008; Dennis Heeney, former financial officer, Alaska Marine Shipping, personal communication with author, October 11, 2008; Carl Moses, former president, Aleut Corp., personal communication with author, October 11, 2008.

34 Taylor Campbell, former captain, Western Pioneer, Inc., personal communication with author, January 17, 2009.

35 Fur Seal Act Amendments of 1983 (16 U.S.C. 1161 et seq.).

36 "Western Pioneer: Stabilizing," *Puget Sound Business Journal* (June 18-24, 1993): 47.

37 "Western Pioneer: Stabilizing," *Puget Sound Business Journal* (June 18-24, 1993): 47; John Wolcott, "Western Pioneer a Bridge Over Oft-Troubled Waters to Alaska," *Puget Sound Business Journal* (June 18-24, 1993): 34.

38 Larry Soriano, president, Western Pioneer, Inc., personal communication with author, March 12, 2009.

39 Taylor Campbell, former captain, Western Pioneer, Inc., personal communication with author, June 25, 2008.

CHAPTER 9

1   Joel Stewart, former captain, Coastal Transportation, Inc., e-mail message to author, September 12, 2008.

2   Joel Stewart, former captain, Coastal Transportation, Inc., e-mail message to author, September 12, 2008.

3   http://www.coastaltrans.com/index.php (accessed April 20, 2012).

4   Guy D. Garcia, "Running Pot Where It's Not as Hot," *Time* (November 29, 1982), http://www.time.com/time/printout/0,8816,955072,00.html (accessed March 3, 2009).

5   Joel Stewart, former captain, Coastal Transportation, Inc., e-mail message to author, September 12, 2008.

6   "Unalaska Has a Lot to Offer Any Business Wanting to Settle in the Aleutians," *Aleutian Times*, June 1985.

7   Advertisement, *Aleutian Times*, June 1985.

8   "Shipping Firm Opens DH Office," *Aleutian Eagle*, September 25, 1986.

9   Hans Mauritzen, former owner, Sunmar Shipping Co., personal communication with author, September 3, 2008.

10 Joel Stewart, former captain, Coastal Transportation, Inc., e-mail message to author, September 12, 2008.

11 "Joint Venture Will Produce Surimi in Dutch," *Aleutian Eagle*, August 1, 1985.

12 Ann Touza, "UniSea: First-Class Seafood," *Alaska Business Monthly* (April 1, 1994), http://www.allbusiness.com/north-america/united-states-alaska/439019-1.html (accessed June 29, 2008); "Production Begins at Great Land," *Aleutian Eagle*, March 27, 1986.

13 "Alyeska Seafoods to Process Surimi in Dutch Harbor," *Aleutian Eagle*, October 24, 1985.

14 "St. Paul's Next Goal Financial Independence via New Port," *Aleutian Eagle*, August 10, 1990.

15 Larry Cotter, CEO, Aleutian Pribilof Island Community Development Association, e-mail message to author, November 4, 2008; "Crab Processing Underway at St. George," *Aleutian Eagle*, February 1, 1991.

16 Neil Rabinowitz, "*Aleutian Mistress* Pioneers Alaska Groundfish Project," *National Fisherman* (November 1981): 110.

17 Helen Jung, "Another Year, Another Fight," *Anchorage Daily News*, August 10, 1997.

18 "Business Notebook," *Anchorage Daily News*, June 7, 1986.

19 National Marine Fisheries Service, "Alaska Pollock," *FishWatch*, http://www.nmfs.noaa.gov/fishwatch/species/walleye_pollock.htm (accessed December 24, 2007).

CHAPTER 10

1   Jacqueline Lindauer, "Exemptions Pose Dilemma for Alaska Delegation," *Aleutian Eagle*, May 4, 1990.

2   Pub. L. No. 98-364, 98 Stat. 450 (July 17, 1984).

3   Jacqueline Lindauer, "Exemptions Pose Dilemma for Alaska Delegation," *Aleutian Eagle*, May 4, 1990; Bill Saporito and Thomas J. Martin, "The Most Dangerous Job in America," *Fortune* (May 31, 1993), http://money.cnn.com/magazines/fortune/fortune_archive/1993/05/31/77905/index.htm (accessed March 15, 2012); National Transportation Safety Board, Safety Recommendation, May 21, 1992.

4   Carol Sturgulewski, "Mosquito Fleet Supported," *Aleutian Eagle*, May 4, 1990.

5   Jacqueline Lindauer, "Exemptions Pose Dilemma for Alaska Delegation," *Aleutian Eagle*, May 4, 1990.

6   City of Unalaska, Resolution No. 90-21, "A Resolution Supporting the Extension of the Fish Tender Vessel General Cargo Exemption," June 14, 1990.

7   Carol Sturgulewski, "City Council Passes Resolution Supporting Mosquito Fleet," *Aleutian Eagle*, June 22, 1990.

8   *Cong. Rec.*, October 27, 1990, H13364.

9   Pub. L. No. 100-424; U.S. Coast Guard, Supplemental Notice of Proposed Rulemaking (SNPRM) in *Federal Register*, October 27, 1992 (57 FR 48672).

10 Aleutian Trade Act of 1990 (P.L. 101-595).

CHAPTER 11

1   Larry Soriano, president, Western Pioneer, Inc., personal communication with author, March 23, 2009.

2   George Collazo, port captain, Coastal Transportation, Inc., personal communication with author, September

2, 2008.

3   "Dock Talk," *Marine Digest and Transportation News* (March 1992): 8.

4   "Western Pioneer: Stabilizing," *Puget Sound Business Journal* (June 18-24, 1993): 47; Tyler Caruso, former port captain, Western Pioneer, Inc., personal communication with author, March 17, 2008.

5   60 FR 54441, October 24, 1995.

6   "Cocaine Seized on Ships in Tory Chief's List," *Observer* (UK), July 18, 1999.

7   John W. Whitney, NOAA Final Report for the *M/V Kuroshima* Response, April 1998; U.S. National Oceanic and Atmospheric Administration, Damage Assessment, Remediation, and Restoration Program, Case: *M/V Kuroshima*, Oil Spill, AK, http://www.darrp.noaa.gov/northwest/kuro/index.html (accessed September 28, 2011).

8   Steve Wilhelm, "Western Pioneer Looks North—and Other Directions," *Puget Sound Business Journal*, June 27, 1997.

9   Larry Soriano, president, Western Pioneer, Inc., personal communication with author, March 16, 2009.

10 Colleen Flood Williams, "Alaska freight just keeps on going and going: freight moving in and out of Alaska moves over mountains, across stormy seas and through glacier-gilded valleys," *Alaska Business Monthly* (March 1, 2004): 60; Larry Soriano, president, Western Pioneer, Inc., personal communication with author, March 16, 2009.

11 Larry Soriano, president, Western Pioneer, Inc., personal communication with author, March 20, 2009.

12 Tom Boyer, "Working Waterfront Losing a Mainstay," *Seattle Times*, June 25, 2005.

CHAPTER 12

1   Frank Norris, "Cargoes North: Containerization and Alaska's Postwar Shipping Crisis," *Alaska History* (Spring 1992): 17.

2   http://www.coastaltransportation.com/vessel-tracking (accessed 6/11/12).

3   "Out-of-Control Fishing Boat Smashes into Five Other Craft," *Seattle Post-Intelligencer*, September 12, 1996; Coastal Transportation, Inc., *Vessel Operation Manual*, 3rd ed. (December 2006), "Collision of the *Mokuhana* at

Pacific Diesel Dock, 11 September 1996," 2-63; "Seven Rescued in High Seas after Leaving Burning Ship," *Seattle Post-Intelligencer*, October 7, 1997.

4   Cahal Milmo, "QE2: Shipwrecked in the Sand," *The Independent* (U.K.), November 12, 2008, http://www.independent.co.uk/news/uk/home-news/qe2-shipwrecked-in-the-sand-1012567.html (accessed 11/12/08).

5   Taylor Campbell, captain, Coastal Transportation, Inc., personal communication with author, October 8, 2008.

6   Arthur Lynch, captain, Coastal Transportation, Inc., personal communication with author, October 9 and October 18, 2008.

7   Based on Marine Stewardship Council Internet home page material, http://www.msc.org/ (accessed March 15, 2012).

8   At-Sea Processors Association press release, "Alaska Pollock Fishery Earns Sustainability Label," June 14, 2004; Mary Pemberton, "Alaska Bering Sea Pollock Gets Eco-label," AP *Worldstream*, October 2, 2004; Unilever press release, "Sustainable Fish Fingers Available in Europe," May 2005; Association of Genuine Alaska Pollock Producers, http://www.alaskapollock.org (accessed March 15, 2012).

9   James N. Ianelli, et al., *Assessment of the walleye pollock stock in the Eastern Bering Sea* (Juneau: National Marine Fisheries Service, December 2011), 85, http://www.afsc.noaa.gov/REFM/docs/2011/EBSpollock.pdf (accessed March 23, 2012); Charles Homans, "Where Have All the Pollock Gone," *Alaska* (June 2008): 26-32, 77. National Marine Fisheries Service, "Fishery summary as of March 23, 2012," http://www.fakr.noaa.gov/sustainablefisheries/reports/outlook.txt (accessed March 23, 2012).

AFTERWORD

1   "Alaskan Progress and Prosperity," *American Review of Reviews* (January 1909): 19.

2   "The Catch About Fish," *The Economist*, (March 19, 1994): 13-14.

Front cover	Taylor Campbell
1-2	Tracy Anderson
6	Pam Aus
8-9	CTI archive
10	Layton Wolf
11a	Taylor Campbell
11b	©Daryl Kyra Lee/AccentAlaska.com
11c-12	Taylor Campbell
14	San Francisco National Maritime Historical Park, G12.797p
16	Archives, University of Alaska Fairbanks
17	NOAA collection
19	University of Washington Libraries, Special Collections, AWC00572
20	Henry W. Elliott, in *Fur-Seal Fisheries of Alaska*, 50th Cong., 2d sess., Ho. Rept. No. 3883, January 29, 1889, Plate 10
21	John E. Thwaites, Archives, University of Alaska Fairbanks
23	Archives, University of Alaska Fairbanks
24	Puget Sound Maritime Historical Society, No. 959
26	John E. Thwaites, Archives, University of Alaska Fairbanks
27-28	Archives, University of Alaska Fairbanks
29	*Seward Gateway,* Dec. 29, 1934
30	Puget Sound Maritime Historical Society
31	John E. Thwaites, Archives, University of Alaska Fairbanks
32	Puget Sound Maritime Historical Society, 3044-7
34	Archives, University of Alaska Fairbanks
35	H. W. May, archival photography by Steve Nicklas, NGS/RSD
36	Alaska State Library, ASL-P134-312-4
37	*Seward Polaris & Kenai Peninsula-Aleutian Chain News,* Jan. 3, 1948
39	Terry Reeve
40	Puget Sound Maritime Historical Society, 6192-1
43	Paul O'Donnell
44	U.S. Naval History and Heritage Command, 19-N-30764
46	Courtesy Frank Buckler, Jr.
52	Puget Sound Maritime Historical Society, 6902
53-55	Taylor Campbell
56	Pam Aus
58	Taylor Campbell
61	Courtesy Jim Mackovjak
63-65	Illustrations by George Collazo
66-67	Pam Aus
68	Taylor Campbell
69-74	Pam Aus
75	MOHAI, SHS10354
77	George Collazo
78a	Pam Aus
78b	Taylor Campbell
78c-81	Pam Aus
82	Taylor Campbell
83	Illustration by George Collazo
84	Leslie Strong
86	Peter Strong
87-88a	CTI archive
88b	Taylor Campbell
88c	CTI archive
88d	Peter Strong
90-91	Courtesy Peter Strong
92-93	Courtesy Mark Dudley
95a-b	Curt Nakon
96	Courtesy Peter Strong
97a	Courtesy Jim Mackovjak
97b-c	Jim Mackovjak
98	Peter Strong
100	Oleg Starchak
103a-b	George Collazo
104	Oleg Starchak
107	Courtesy Jim Mackovjak
108a	Curt Nakon
108b	CTI archive
108c	Curt Nakon
108d	CTI archive
110	George Collazo
112	CTI archive
114	Archives, University of Alaska Fairbanks
115	Cecil Yates
116	Illustrations by George Collazo
118	Courtesy Peter Strong
121	Taylor Campbell
136	Tracy Anderson

I would like to acknowledge the many individuals whose selfless labor and gifts have gone into the creation of this book and who have helped make Coastal Transportation what it is today. Although this is certainly not a comprehensive list, my heartfelt thanks are extended to:

First of all the author, Jim Mackovjak, whom I met 40 years ago, in the summer of 1972, in Petersburg, Alaska. We were then both rookie engineers on cannery tenders employed by Petersburg Fisheries, the predecessor of Icicle Seafoods. Next, Bob Thorstenson, who always believed in both Jim and me. Also Chuck Bundrant and Trident Seafoods, Coastal's first customer, who encouraged us as a fledgling transportation company and whose support continues today. Next, my father and mother, Dennis and Vera Strong, who gave me the skills and wisdom, as a sometimes rambunctious firstborn son, to understand the world we live in. Especially the loyal employees of Coastal Transportation, whose dedication and hard work make the company better every day. And our loyal customers in Seattle and the many rural communities in Western Alaska, whose patience and understanding of the constantly changing weather conditions allow us to continue service in one of the most challenging places on earth. I also give thanks to our Lord, who gives us the ability to persevere through the ups and downs of life.

Finally, my dedicated and wonderful wife of 35 years, Leslie. We met in Cordova, Alaska, in 1975 during salmon season on the Copper River. Her knowledge of the industry and her encouragement to pursue my interest in transportation helped form Coastal Transportation in 1984. Her support continues to this day, as Leslie is my confidante, my best friend, and a true partner in the work.

Peter D. Strong
Seattle, Washington
May 2012